Happy Birthday
Ma
Love June &
Dana
2007

*f*P

STANDING IN THE

A Celebration
of Black Prayer

THE SCHOMBURG CENTER FOR
RESEARCH IN BLACK CULTURE,
THE NEW YORK PUBLIC LIBRARY

FOREWORD BY
CORETTA SCOTT KING

FREE PRESS
New York
London
Toronto
Sydney
Singapore

FREE PRESS
A Division of Simon & Schuster, Inc.
1230 Avenue of the Americas
New York, NY 10020

For information about special discounts for bulk purchases, please contact Simon & Schuster Special Sales: 1-800-456-6798 or business@simonandschuster.com

Designed by Joel Avirom and Jason Snyder

Manufactured in Hong Kong

10 9 8 7 6 5 4 3 2 1

Library of Congress Cataloging-in-Publication Data

Standing in the need of prayer: a celebration of Black prayer / by the Schomburg Center for Research in
    Black Culture, the New York Public Library; foreword by Coretta Scott King.
        p. cm.
    Includes index.
        1. African Americans—Prayer-books and devotions—English. I. Schomburg Center for Research in
Black Culture.

    BL625.2.S73 2003
    291.4 33 08996073—dc21

                                                                                2003051618

ISBN: 0-7432-3466-9

TO THE ANCESTORS,
WHOSE PRAYERS AND STRUGGLES CREATED
OUR ROAD TO VICTORY.

God of our weary years,
God of our silent tears,
Thou who hast brought us thus far on the way;
Thou who hast by thy might,
Led us into the light,
Keep us forever in the path, we pray.

—JAMES WELDON JOHNSON

Ain't my brother or my sister
but it's me, oh, Lord,
Standing in the need of prayer.
Ain't my brother or my sister
but it's me, oh, Lord,
Standing in the need of prayer.
It's me, it's me, oh, Lord,
Standing in the need of prayer.
It's me, it's me, oh, Lord,
Standing in the need of prayer.

—AFRICAN-AMERICAN SPIRITUAL

FOREWORD
Coretta Scott King

Throughout the epic freedom struggle of African Americans, our great sustainer of hope has been the power of prayer. We prayed for deliverance in a dozen African languages, chained to the holds of slave ships, on the auction block, in the fields of oppression, and under the lash. We prayed when we "followed the drinking gourd" on the Underground Railroad. We prayed when our families were torn asunder by the slave traders. We prayed when our homes and churches were burned and bombed and when our people were lynched by racist mobs. So many times it seemed our prayers went unanswered, but we kept faith that one day our unearned suffering would prove to be redemptive.

This remarkable collection of prayers, accompanied by moving illustrations, includes many of the most poignant prayers uttered throughout the African diaspora and down through the centuries. It includes the spiritual "Precious Lord, Take My Hand," a favorite of my husband, Martin Luther King, Jr. The prayers in these pages come from gospel lyrics and popular song, literature and poetry, and sacred scriptures. There are prayers from myriad traditions, including Haitian Vodou, Buddhism, Yoruba, and Islam, as well as Christianity. And then there are the marvelous photographs of people praying in their homes; in churches, mosques, and temples; in prison and outdoor meetings. There is even a photo of my husband leading a Christian prayer at our dinner table, under a portrait of one of his mentors, Mohandas K. Gandhi, a Hindu.

As a young child growing up in Marion, Alabama, I remember my pastor at Mt. Tabor Church responding to the racial abuse of one of our congregation by saying, "God loves us all, and people will reap what they sow. . . . So just keep on praying. Don't worry. God will straighten things out." I believed he was right then, and I believe it still.

My parents made sure that prayer would be a regular part of my life, and it has been to this very day. Prayer is how we open our hearts to God, how we make that vital connection that empowers us to overcome overwhelming obstacles and become instruments of God's will. And despite the pain and suffering that I have experienced and that comes to all of our lives, I am more convinced than ever before that prayer gives us strength and hope, a sense of divine companionship, as we struggle for justice and righteousness.

Prayer was a wellspring of strength and inspiration during the Civil Rights Movement. Throughout the movement, we prayed for greater human understanding. We prayed for the safety of our compatriots in the freedom struggle. We prayed for victory in our nonviolent protests, for brotherhood and sisterhood among people of all races, for reconciliation and the fulfillment of the Beloved Community.

For my husband, Martin Luther King, Jr., prayer was a daily source of courage and strength that gave him the ability to carry on in even the darkest hours of our struggle. I remember one very difficult day when he came home bone-weary from the stress that came with his leadership of the Montgomery Bus Boycott. In the middle of that night, he was awakened by a threatening and abusive phone call, one of many we received throughout the movement. On this particular occasion, however, Martin had had enough.

After the call, he got up from bed and made himself some coffee. He began to worry about his family, and all of the burdens that came with our movement weighed heavily on his soul. With his head in his hands, Martin bowed over the kitchen table and prayed aloud to God: "Lord, I am taking a stand for what I believe is right. The people are looking to me for leadership, and if I stand before them without strength and courage, they will falter. I am at the end of my powers. I have nothing left. I have come to the point where I can't face it alone."

Later he told me, "At that moment, I experienced the presence of the Divine as I had never experienced Him before. It seemed as though I could hear a voice saying: 'Stand up for righteousness; stand up for truth; and God will be at your side forever.'" When Martin stood up from the table, he was imbued with a new sense of confidence, and he was ready to face anything.

I believe that this prayer was a critical turning point for the African-American freedom struggle, because from that point forward, we had a leader who was divinely inspired and could not be turned back by threats or any form of violence. This kind of courage and conviction is truly contagious, and I know his example inspired me to carry on through the difficult days of my journey.

A few nights after Martin's moment of truth, I had mine. I was sitting in my living room in Montgomery, chatting with a friend, while my new baby daughter, Yolanda, was asleep in the back room. Suddenly, we heard a loud thump on the front porch. Because of all the recent threats, I urged my friend to get up. "It sounds as if someone has hit the house. We'd better move to the back."

As we moved toward the back, we felt a thunderous blast, followed by shattering glass and billowing smoke. I hurried to Yolanda's room and thanked God that she was all right. I called the church where my husband was speaking, but he was addressing the audience at the time. He called me back shortly afterward as a large crowd gathered at our house, and then he rushed home.

The crowd was angry at what had happened, and there was a lot of tension between the police and those who had gathered, some of whom were armed with guns, rocks, and bottles. In the midst of all of the turmoil, I said a silent prayer for the protection of our family and the restoration of peace. Then Martin began to speak to the crowd from the front porch of our home. "My wife and baby are all right," he said. "I want you to go home and put down your weapons. We cannot solve this problem through retaliatory violence. We must meet violence with nonviolence."

As Martin continued to speak, I was enveloped by a growing calm. "God is with us," I thought. "God is truly with us." The fear and anger around me began to melt like the receding snows of spring. Almost at that moment, Martin concluded his remarks to the crowd: "Remember, if I am stopped, this movement will not stop, because God is with this movement. Go home with this glowing faith and this radiant assurance."

Martin's speech on that day was yet another crucial turning point for our freedom struggle because it set the tone of nonviolence that gave our movement its unique credibility and enabled all of the victories we achieved under his leadership.

From that day on, I was fully prepared for my role as Martin's wife and partner in the struggle. There would be many more days of difficulty and worry, and there would be many more prayers. But the unwavering belief that we were doing

God's work became a daily source of faith and courage that undergirded our freedom movement.

It is said that every prayer is heard and every prayer is answered in some way, and I believe this is true for people of all faiths. I still believe that the millions of prayers spoken by African Americans from the Middle Passage on down to today have been heard by a righteous and loving God.

This wonderful book you hold in your hands is itself a blessing, because it reveals the power of prayer to transform our lives and help provide the spiritual depth that is needed to make us whole. Keep it near so you can reach out and be uplifted and inspired during the challenging passages of your journey. Know in your heart and soul that our faith and our prayers, so beautifully illustrated in the words and images in these pages, will surely be redeemed, and the Beloved Community will become a glowing reality.

STANDING IN THE NEED OF PRAYER

INTRODUCTION

Howard Dodson,
Director of the Schomburg Center
for Research in Black Culture

I was born in Chester, Pennsylvania, a small industrial town just south of Philadelphia, and raised in a Christian home where prayer was part of my daily regimen. At home, we said grace before every meal and prayed before going to bed. During elementary school, we recited the Lord's Prayer as part of our morning exercises along with the Pledge of Allegiance to the flag. At Bethany Baptist Church, prayer was the most repeated and reinforcing ritual of the service. There was a prayer to open the service, a prayer before each offering (there were usually two or three), a prayer before the sermon, a prayer before or after the pastor opened the doors of the church for new members, a prayer before communion (if it was communion Sunday), and a prayer to conclude the service. Baptists believe in the efficacy and power of prayer. I learned to believe, too.

Over the course of the last few decades, I have traveled extensively, visiting black communities in Africa, Latin America, the Caribbean, and throughout the United States. I have also had an opportunity to study the black religious experience throughout the world. I have discovered that Baptists are not the only ones who believe in the efficacy and power of prayer. African peoples in the United States and around the world communicate with God and other invisible forces of the universe—including the dead, the ancestors, and the unborn—through a variety of sacred rituals, rites, and ceremonies that use sacrifices, offerings, and the pouring of libations to link communicants' spiritual and physical worlds. But no single act of worship is more pervasive in African-American and African diasporan religious (and secular) life than prayer, a petition or other form of address to God or other forces of the spiritual world through word or thought. Indeed, according to John S. Mbiti, a leading historian of African religion, "prayer, more than any other aspect of religion, contains the most intense expression of African traditional spirituality."

Most of the African captives who were enslaved in the Americas came from West and Central Africa, a vast area comprised of literally thousands of ethnic, national, religious, and cultural groups. As a consequence, it is difficult to make broad general statements about their religious and spiritual lives. In many areas of West Africa, Islam had established a major religious presence by the fourteenth century, prior to the advent of the transatlantic slave trade. Muslims were among those captured, enslaved, and transported to the Americas. They brought their West African Islamic traditions with them to the Americas. Among the most frequently recorded rituals were the daily prayers. Practicing Muslims among the enslaved African population continued the practice of praying five times a day. Facing the east, kneeling (preferably on a prayer rug), and pressing their foreheads to the ground, they offered up their daily prayers to Allah, the Magnificent, the Merciful.

There is some evidence that European Christian missionaries had made some inroads into West Africa by the mid-fifteenth century prior to the advent of the slave trade as well. It is likely that some of the Africans transported to the Americas were Christian (probably Catholic) converts.

The vast majority of the Africans enslaved in the Americas, however, were from traditional African societies and practiced their traditional religions. And while it is true that there was tremendous ethnic, national, and religious diversity among West and Central African people, their religious and spiritual worlds included a number of common beliefs, worldviews, and practices. Most believed in a Supreme Being, a benevolent, transcendent God, creator of the world and everything in it. They believed in numerous lesser gods or divinities who governed natural forces and phenomena and intervened in the affairs of humankind. They believed that their ancestors—both those who died long ago and those of recent memory—were a special class of spirits who, as custodians of custom and law, also had the power to intervene in the day-to-day affairs of the society. Many believed that spirits dwelled in trees and other living objects and were capable of granting peoples' wishes. In most traditional African societies, priests served as intermediaries, leading worship and ritual sacrifices to the gods and the spirits and honoring the gods, the spirits, and the ancestors. Generally, the gods had altars, shrines, or temples dedicated to their worship. Frequently, the priests were also skilled diviners and healers. Finally, most believed in spirit possession, in which devotees became mediums of their gods, entered into states of trance, and danced out of the character of a god, including becoming its mouthpiece.

The rituals, ceremonies, and rites that comprised traditional African worship varied considerably, but virtually all included drumming, dancing, and singing. Individual and collective prayers and sacrifices were also central to all worship services. The power of the gods and the spirits in traditional West and Central African societies was present on every level—cosmic, national, social, individual, and environmental. The well-being of each individual and the society as a whole derived from the close relationship of humankind to the gods, the ancestors, and the spirits.

The traditional religions, beliefs, rituals, and worship practices did not survive intact among the enslaved Africans who crossed the Atlantic. Enough did survive, however, to permit enslaved Africans to lay the foundations for a variety of New World African religious practices. These New World African religious forms were strongest in Latin America and the Caribbean in Candomblé (Brazil), Santería (Cuba), Shango (Trinidad), and Vodou (Haiti), where the traditional West and Central African worldview and perspectives were adapted to their New World environments. The most obvious continuity between traditional African religions and their New World surrogates is the style of ritual performance. Drumming, singing, and dancing are essential features of all of these New World religions and are crucial to ceremonial possession of devotees by their gods. And the phenomenon of possession is the climax of the service in each one of these religions. Prayers and sacrifices to the gods are also pervasive in these New World African religions. While being syntheses of traditions from several West and Central African societies, the prayers and other rites, rituals, and practices created by enslaved Africans in the Americas are nevertheless unique products of the American environment.

Christianity established a strong presence among enslaved Africans and their descendants in the Americas. In Latin America and the Caribbean, Spanish and Portuguese Catholic missionaries introduced the Roman Catholic traditions to enslaved Africans. In some areas, traditional African rites and rituals have been incorporated into Catholic practices by enslaved Africans and their descendants.

Enslaved Africans in the United States, on the other hand, were proselytized by Protestant Christian missionaries. Methodists and Baptists were most prevalent among enslaved Africans, but they eventually practiced in virtually all American denominations—Presbyterian, Episcopalian, and others. In Baptist and

Methodist traditions, with which the vast majority of enslaved Africans in the United States kept faith, something else happened. Dissatisfied with both the content and the style of religious worship presented by white Christians, enslaved Africans appropriated the Christian gospel and rituals and incorporated traditional African performance styles into them. In prayer meetings and other secret worship services held at night in the woods, in praise houses and "hush hollows," far removed from the eyes and influence of whites, enslaved Africans invented new forms of Christian religious practice that drew much of its unique essence from traditional African religions. Gone were the traditional African languages and rituals. But into their new language and Christian religion they brought the spirit, the practices, and the performance styles of traditional African religions. New African-American Christian religions emerged.

Today the overwhelming majority of African-American Christians in the United States are Baptists. Methodist and Pentecostal groups are next, followed by the other dominant American Protestant religious groups. African Americans in the United States also worship in the Ethiopian Orthodox Church, one of the founding Christian churches in the world (it dates from the fourth century A.D.). Since slavery, they have founded literally thousands of Christian religious sects, joined white Protestant and Catholic churches, and become practicing Baha'i, Hindus, Jews, and Buddhists. They also worship in several Islamic traditions and practice many of the New World African religions. The religious world of people of African descent living in the United States is extremely diverse. But prayer is a central part of all of their religious practices.

Standing in the Need of Prayer is a reminder of the way prayer has changed the lives of African peoples. Comprising some one hundred photographs and an equal number of prayer texts drawn principally from the collections of the Schomburg Center for Research in Black Culture, this book is a testament to the centrality of prayer in African-American and African diasporan life and religious practice. It is also an expression of the belief held widely among people of African descent that they can invoke God's presence through prayer and that prayer changes things. Through these selected images and prayer texts, we learn when, where, how, and under what circumstances people of African descent from diverse religious backgrounds invoke the presence of God in their lives and in their world.

The prayer texts included in *Standing in the Need of Prayer* have been selected from a wide variety of sources. Some are by ministers, priests, and other religious leaders. Some are taken from sacred texts—the Bible, the Qur'ân, etc. Some are familiar prayers and meditations that have been set to music. Prayers by famous African Americans—W. E. B. Du Bois, James Baldwin, James Weldon Johnson, and Marian Wright Edelman—are included here. Other prayer texts are humble supplications of anonymous practitioners of their respective faiths.

Photographers whose work is included here range from *New York Times* photographer Chester Higgins, Jr., to photographer Gordon Parks and photographer and artist Coreen Simpson. While the names of the vast majority of the subjects in these photographs are unknown, there are moving images of public personages such as Malcolm X, Martin Luther King, Jr., Florence Griffith-Joyner, Mary McLeod Bethune, and Calvin Butts. All are seen at moments when they were in the midst of a prayer ritual.

Several members of the staff at the Schomburg Center have been instrumental in making this book possible. Staff editor Jacqueline Dowdell and staff researcher

Christopher Moore identified images with the assistance of the Center's Curator of Photographs and Prints, Mary Yearwood. They also located prayer texts with the assistance of Assistant Director Roberta Yancy. Moore, Dowdell, and Yancy matched images with text and provided overall editorial supervision. Andrea Au coordinated the project on behalf of Simon & Schuster and kept us on schedule. A special word of thanks to Mrs. Coretta Scott King for writing the foreword to this book.

The Schomburg Center is pleased to offer you *Standing in the Need of Prayer*. It is hoped that it will remind each of us that we are all children of God and that His presence is central to our lives in all of our religious traditions. It is an invitation to all who read and study it to know God, whatever your choice of religion may be, and to believe in God and to keep God in your lives through prayer.

Dear Father . . . we come before You on our knees this evening to ask You to watch over us and hold back the hand of the destroying angel. Lord, sprinkle the doorpost of this house with the blood of the Lamb to keep all the wicked men away. Lord, we praying for every mother's son and daughter everywhere in the world but we want You to take special care of this girl here tonight, Lord, and don't let no evil come nigh her. We know You's able to do it, Lord, in Jesus' name, Amen.

—JAMES BALDWIN
FROM GO TELL IT ON THE MOUNTAIN

RICHARD SAUNDERS

Gracious God, we come before you with thanksgiving that our [child] is developing his own relationship with you. We pray that your Holy Spirit will guide him and that he may come to know and love you as heavenly parent and faithful friend. O God, we pray that he will have discernment to know your will and courage to follow your will for his life. Keep him, dear God, even as Jesus prayed that you would keep the disciples and the church.

—WILLIAM D. WATLEY
"FAITH"

RICHARD SAUNDERS

Heavenly Father, help me to cast my cares upon you, to take time to pray, and be renewed each day in the healing waters of godly fellowship. Amen.

—Joann Stevens
"A Sisterly Celebration"
from Sister to Sister Devotions for
and from African American Women

In the name of the Father, the Son and the Holy Spirit, One God, Amen. We believe and offer our supplications unto the Holy Trinity. We denounce Satan in the sight of the Holy Mother Orthodox Church. And in the presence of the Virgin Mary whom is Zion for ever and ever. Amen.

—ETHIOPIAN ORTHODOX TEWAHEDO PRAYER

SULAIMAN ELLISON

15

We are here this evening, Jesus
    Oh yeah
We can't do nothing without you
    Uh huh
Come Holy Spirit, Heavenly Dove
    Oh yeah
With all thou quickening power
    Power!

—James Brown
"You Know the Purpose
of Our Gathering, Jesus"

GILBERTO WILSON

Those who believe, and work righteousness, their Lord will guide them because of their Faith: beneath them will flow rivers in Gardens of Bliss. (This will be) their prayer therein: "Glory to Thee, O Allah!" and "Peace" will be their greeting therein. And the close of their prayer will be: "Praise be to Allah, the Cherisher and Sustainer of the Worlds!"

—QUR'ÂN, CHAPTER 10: 9–10

Love that is of God encourages growth and models
healthy relationships. Yes, love that is of God is stubborn,
forgiving, and unconditional—not just when the object of
that love is the other but also when the object is the self.
This is how our daughters will begin to learn of God's love.
Beloved, let us love our daughters as God has loved us.

—Reverend Emma Jordan-Simpson
"Loving Our Daughters"

May you be for us a moon of joy and happiness.
Let the young become strong and the grown man
maintain his strength, the pregnant woman be delivered
and the woman who has given birth suckle her child.
Let the stranger come to the end of his journey and those
who remain at home dwell safely in their houses. Let the
flocks that go to feed in the pastures return happily. May
you be a moon of harvest and of calves. May you be a
moon of restoration and of good health.

—"BE FOR US A MOON OF JOY"
TRADITIONAL ETHIOPIAN PRAYER

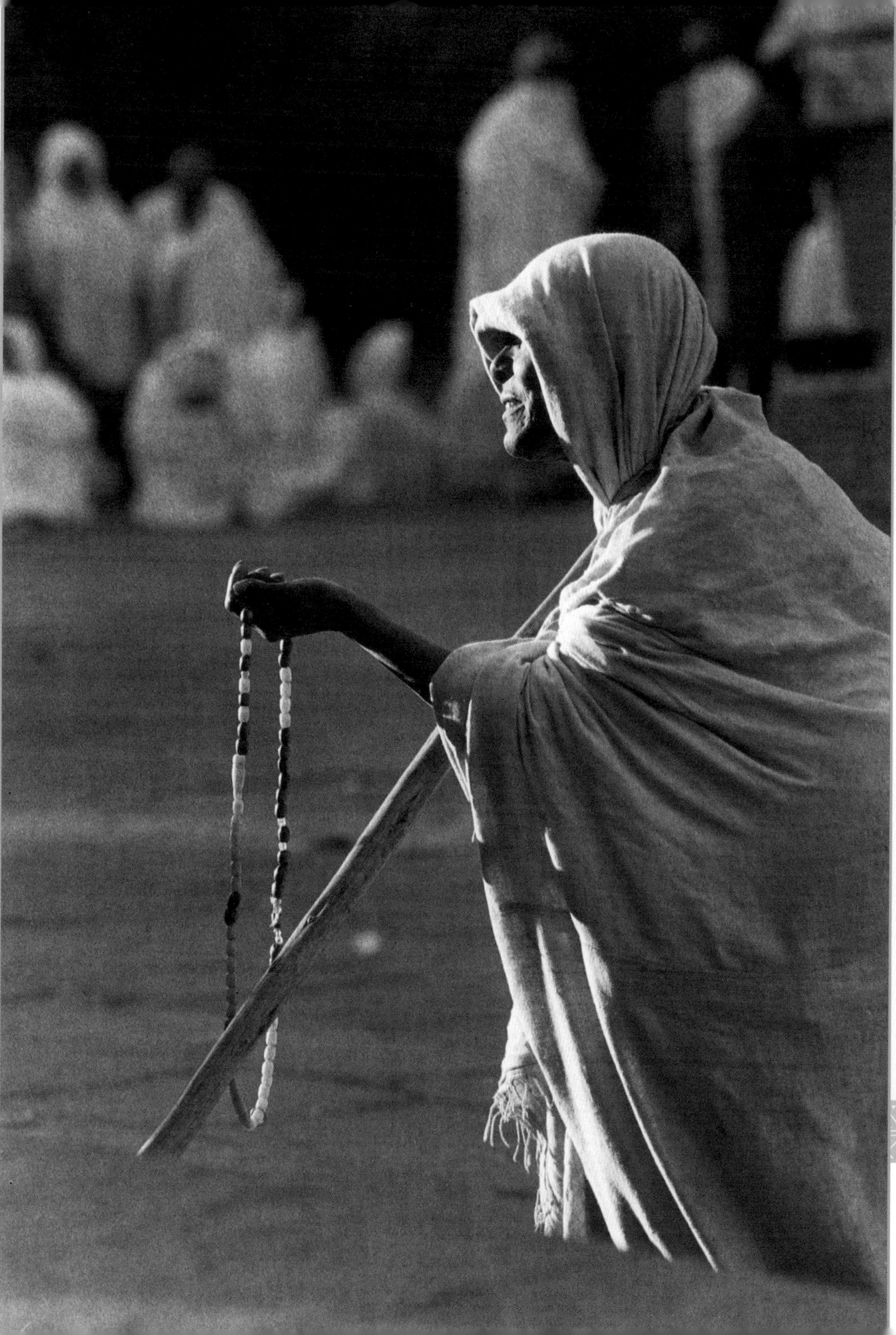

SULAIMAN ELLISON

In the Name of Allah, the Beneficent, the Merciful.
Praise be to Allah, The Lord of the Worlds,
The Beneficent, the Merciful,
Master of the day of Requital.
Thee do we serve and Thee do we beseech for help.
Guide us on the right path, the path of those upon whom
    Thou hast bestowed favours,
Not those upon whom wrath is brought down,
    Nor those who go astray.

—AL-FATIHAH (THE OPENING)
CHAPTER 1:1–7 OF THE QUR'ÂN

We ask for the knowledge of the Healing
    of our bodies
We know that knowledge is healing
And healing is knowledge.
As we seek knowledge
We ask that you would help us
To find and use this knowledge
to become stronger in our mission. . . .

—Reverend Lillie Kate Benitez
"A Prayer for the Healing of the Body"

Yeahhh! Thou balm in Gilead. You're a balm in Gilead. And we call Your Name because earth has no sorrow that heaven cannot heal. Heal! Let virtue go-out-on-ether-waves! Let healing virtue go in every hospital. Let the healing virtue go out.

Heeealll!

Saaave!

Lift!

Healll!

Move oppression!

Lift the Burden.

Move obsession!

Move possession! in Jesus' Name.

—RICHARD DANIEL HENTON
"A PRAYER FOR HEALING"

29

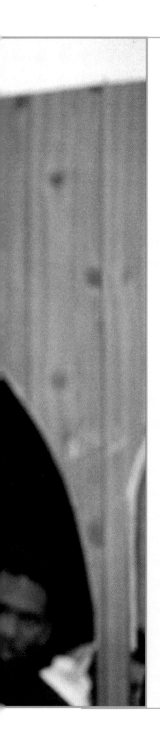

And it shall come to pass in the last days, saith
God, I will pour out my spirit upon all flesh. And
your sons and your daughters shall prophesy and
your young men shall see visions, and your old
men shall dream dreams. Yes, I will endue even my
slaves, both men and women, with a portion of
my spirit, and they shall prophesy. And I will
show portents in the sky above, and signs on the
earth below—blood and fire and drifting smoke.
The sun shall be turned to darkness, and the moon
to blood, before that great, resplendent day, the day
of the Lord, shall come. And then everyone who
invokes the name of the Lord shall be saved.

—ACTS 2:17–19

My shepherd is the living Lord,
Now shall my wants be well supplied,
His providence and holy word
Becomes my safety and my guide.

In pastures where salvation grows,
He makes me food—he makes me rest—
There living water gently flows,
And all the food divinely blessed. . . .

Though I walk through the gloomy vale,
Where death and all its terrors are,
My heart and hope shall never fail:
For God, my Shepherd's with me there.

—ISAAC WATTS
"MY SHEPHERD IS THE LIVING LORD"

DORIS ULMANN

STEVE HART

O God of Harriet Tubman
and Sojourner Truth
of Frederick Douglass and
Booker T. Washington
of George Washington Carver
and Mary McLeod Bethune,
Be with Your Black sons
and daughters today.
O God of Martin Luther King
and Malcolm X
of James Baldwin and Fannie Lou Hamer
of Howard Thurman and Benjamin Mays,
Be with Your Black children today.

—MARIAN WRIGHT EDELMAN
"PRAYER FOR THE BLACK CHILD"

For the Lord himself shall descend from heaven with a shout, with the voice of the archangel, and with the trumpet of God: and the dead in Christ shall rise first. Then we which are alive and remain shall be caught up together with them in the clouds, to meet the Lord in the air: and so shall we ever be with the Lord. Wherefore comfort one another with these words.

—1 Thessalonians 4:16–18

Precious Lord, take my hand,
Lead me on, let me stand,
I am tired, I am weak, I am worn
Thru the storm, thru the night,
Lead me on to the light,
Take my hand, precious Lord,
Lead me home.
When my way grows drear, precious Lord, linger near,
When my life is almost gone,
Hear my cry, hear my call,
Hold my hand lest I fall;
Take my hand, precious Lord,
Lead me home.
When the darkness appears and the night draws near,
And the day is past and gone,
At the river I stand,
Guide my feet, hold my hand;
Take my hand, precious Lord,
Lead me home.

—THOMAS ANDREW DORSEY
"PRECIOUS LORD, TAKE MY HAND"

The kindness of the Mother!

—Greeting of Oxum

LAWRENCE N. SHUSTAK

42

Do not envy the oppressor,
And choose none of his ways;
For the perverse person is an abomination
    to the Lord,
But His secret counsel is with the upright.
The curse of the Lord is on the house
    of the wicked,
But He blesses the home of the just.
Surely He scorns the scornful,
But gives grace to the humble.
The wise shall inherit glory,
But shame shall be the legacy of fools.

—Proverbs 3:31–35

Free at last, free at last,
Thank God Almighty, I'm free at last.

The very time I thought I was lost,
Thank God Almighty, I'm free at last;
My dungeon shook and my chains fell off,
Thank God Almighty, I'm free at last.
This is religion, I do know,
Thank God Almighty, I'm free at last;
For I never felt such a love before,
Thank God Almighty, I'm free at last.

—AFRICAN-AMERICAN SPIRITUAL

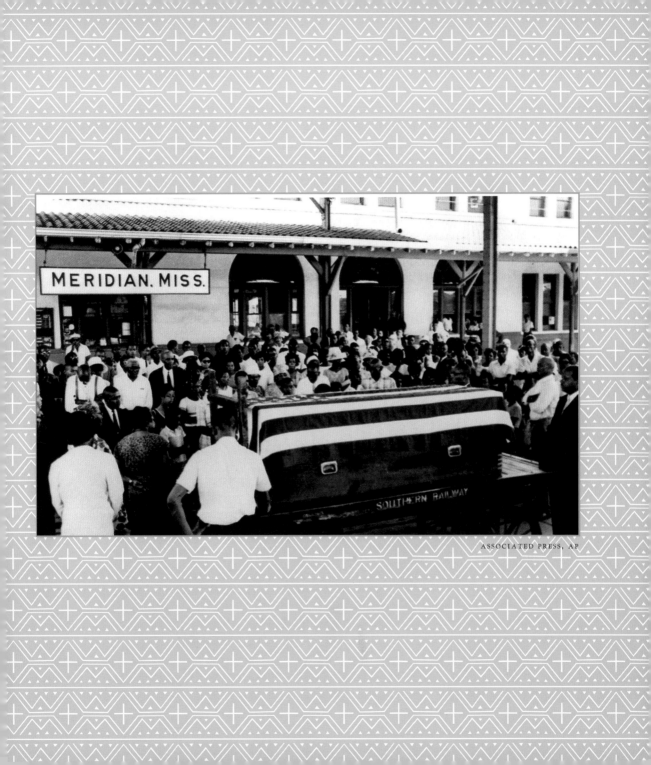

MERIDIAN, MISS.

SOUTHERN RAILWAY

BEVERLY CONLEY

Defend Lord,
these Thy children
in all their work
and all their prayer.
Spread among them the desire to know
and learn and do.
Let them grow in the capacity
for worthy work and in all their working and thinking let them
not forget the host of witnesses about them—those that
love and those that inspire—and may they in the end
prove worthy of their great heritage.
Amen.

—W. E. B. Du Bois
from *Prayers for Dark People*

STEVE HART

48

The Lord is in His holy temple;
The Lord is on His heavenly throne.
He observes the sons of men;
His eyes examine them.
The Lord examines the righteous,
But the wicked and those who love violence His soul hates.
On the wicked He will rain fiery coals and burning sulfur;
A scorching wind will be their lot.
For the Lord is righteous,
He loves justice;
Upright men will see His face.

—PSALM 11:4–7

Father, I stretch my hands to Thee,
No other help I know;
If Thou withdraw Thyself from me,
Ah! whither shall I go?
What did Thine only Son endure,
Before I drew my breath!
What pain, what labor to secure
My soul from endless death!
Surely Thou canst not let me die,
O speak and I shall live;
And here I will unwearied lie,
Till Thou Thy spirit give.
Author of faith! To Thee I lift
my weary, longing eyes;
O let me now receive that gift!
My soul without it dies.

—CHARLES WESLEY
"FATHER I STRETCH MY HANDS TO THEE"

Blessed is one who sits in the hands of
the Amen Ra for it is He who directs the timid,
who rescues the humble and the needy,
who gives the breath of life to the one who
He loves and grants him or her a long life in the
West of Thebes.

—Translation of Egyptian incantation from the Husia

Wade in the water,
Wade in the water children,
Wade in the water,
God's gonna trouble the water.
If you don't believe I've been redeemed,
Just follow me down to Jordan's stream,
God's gonna trouble the water.

—"WADE IN THE WATER,"
AN AFRICAN-AMERICAN SPIRITUAL, CA. 1800

BOB GORE

When we walk with the Lord, in the light of His Word,
What a glory He sheds on our way!
While we do His good will He abides with us still,
And with all who will trust and obey.
Trust and obey.
For there's no other way.

—John H. Sammis
"Trust and Obey," ca. 1887

O God of all children of Somalia, Sarajevo, South Africa,
    and South Carolina
Of Albania, Alabama, Bosnia, and Boston,
Of Cracow and Cairo, Chicago and Croatia,
Help us to love and respect
and protect them all.
O God of Black and Brown and White and Albino children
        and all those mixed together,
Of children who are rich and poor
        and in between,
Of children who speak English and Spanish and Russian
        and Hmong and languages
our ears cannot discern,
Help us to love and respect
and protect them all.

—Marian Wright Edelman
"Prayers for All Our Children"

Lord, the psalmist asked, how long O Lord,
how long will Thou hide Thyself from me.
Today, God, there are terrible disasters
which take the lives of many people.
It is hard to recognize Your hand in such a tragedy,
but I pray that through such tribulations, many people can come
to a deepened relationship with You,
even a new relationship with You,
as we recognize the frailty of our physical existence
and the lack of control we have over it.
Perhaps You use these opportunities to knock at the hearts
of those affected by these calamities, and I pray they let You in.
    No matter what tribulations arise in this life,
if we have You dwelling in our hearts,
we are sure to overcome. In Christ's Name.
Amen.

—Reverend Chestina Mitchell Archibald
"In the Wake of Tragedy"

Father, we thank Thee that
Thou are our Father.
We commit ourselves to Thee.
May Thy spirit of absolute purity,
absolute honesty, absolute unselfishness,
    absolute love permeate our lives. May we join
    our hands and our hearts with the peoples of
    the world to build a fellowship
of freedom, of peace, of love,
of brotherhood everywhere.
Amen.

—MARY MCLEOD BETHUNE
"MY PRAYER"

So then, just talk about "spiritual color" and tell them:
"Whatever color love is, that's the color of God;
whatever color justice is, that's the color of God;
whatever color peace is, that's the color of God;
whatever color freedom is, that's the color of God;
whatever color joy is, that's the color of God;
whatever color healing is, that's the color of God;
whatever color salvation is, that's the color of God;
whatever color power is, that's the color of God;
whatever color truth is, that's the color of God."
So then, regardless of who we are or where we come from,
regardless of our own skin color or racial identity,
we should strive to be God's (spiritual) color. Amen.

—KENNETH WATERS
"MADE IN GOD'S IMAGE"

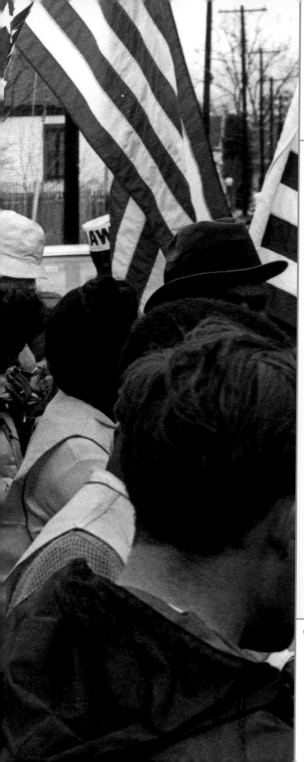

We are made in the image of God, African Americans, as well as all others. From one blood has God created all the races and nations of the earth. . . .

We are thankful for Rosa Parks, Medgar Evers, James Farmer, and Fannie Lou Hamer. Nothing could quench their thirst for freedom. It was their time and they would not be denied. . . .

May God help us to exercise more seriously our right to vote and our pursuit of equality. God strengthen us in the ongoing struggle for freedom, civil rights, and justice.

—CIVIL RIGHTS PRAYER
FROM THE
AFRICAN AMERICAN HERITAGE HYMNAL

O mother, we beseech thee to
Deliver us,
Look after us,
Look after our children;
Thou who art established at Ado.

—TRADITIONAL YORUBA PRAYER

69

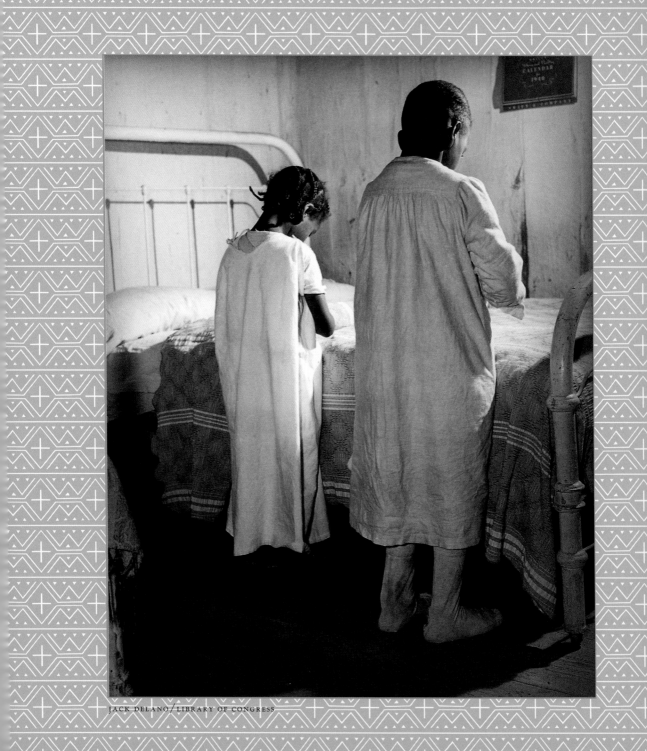

When I'm through with all the day,
And I kneel at night to pray—
God sees.
After I am gone to bed,
If I cover up my head—
God sees.
Even when I'm sound asleep,
While the angels 'round me creep—
God sees.
So you see I never fear,
God's protection's ever near—
God sees.

—FRANK BARBOUR COFFIN
"GOD SEES"

When the Qur'ân is read, listen to it with attention, and hold your peace: that ye may receive Mercy.

And do thou (O reader!) bring thy Lord to remembrance in thy (very) soul, with humility and in reverence, without loudness in words, in the mornings and evenings; and be not thou of those who are unheedful.

—QUR'ÂN, CHAPTER 7: 204–5

COREEN SIMPSON

Rising above every other need, O heavenly Father, is our great need for Thee. More than our bodies need food, and drink, and clothing, and shelter, do our souls need to feast and find refreshment upon Thee, and to feel Thy righteousness wrapped around us as our garment, and to find shelter and peace for our souls in the refuge of eternity, Thou great Rock of Ages.

—RALPH MARK GILBERT
"OUR NEED FOR THEE"

Hear me, dear Jesus While I pray to Thee;
Bow down Thine ear in mercy—
Grant my fervent plea;
Fill with Thy grace and power
Every passing hour;
Draw me, dear Jesus, draw me
And I'll run after Thee.
Guide me, dear Jesus, guide me
All along my way;
Thou art my strong Deliverer—
Help me, Lord, I pray;
Make me to ever follow, Hard after Thee;
Draw me, dear Jesus, draw me
And I'll run after Thee.

—GARFIELD THOMAS HAYWOOD
"DRAW ME, DEAR JESUS"

STEVE HART

77

Please, don't leave me, don't leave me, Jesus.
Don't leave me, don't leave me, Lord.
I don't believe that God would bring me,
I don't believe that God would bring me,
I don't believe that God would bring me
 this far just to leave me.

       —CURTIS BURRELL
     "I DON'T FEEL NO WAYS TIRED"

Now, great God, give us thy power to believe in ourselves,
and in what we can do, and in what we can be, and in what we are.
May the grace of Jesus Christ be with us all. Amen.

—Leon H. Sullivan
"A Prayer for a Positive Attitude"

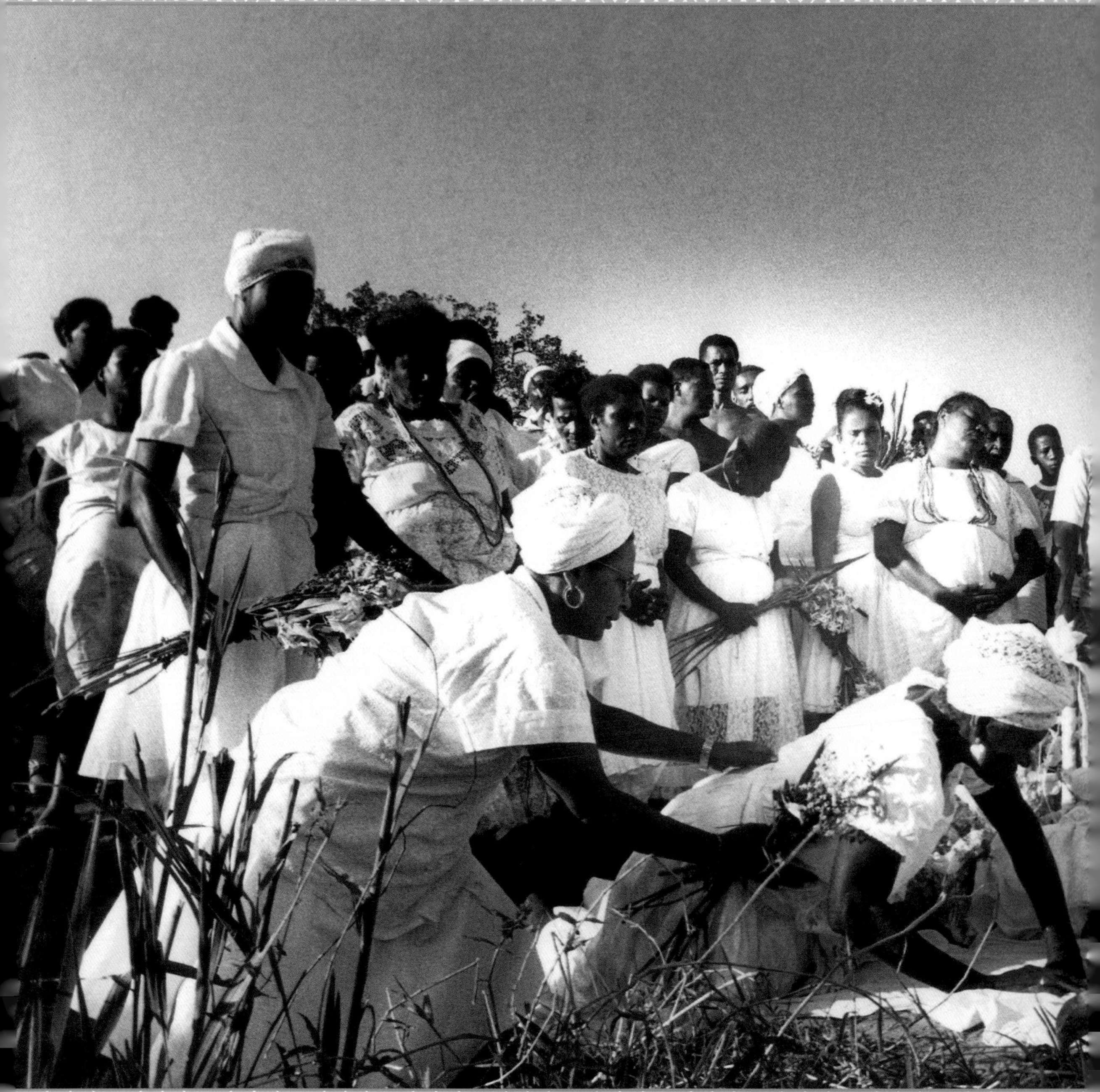

Invoking these laws
I implore you Eshu
to plant in my mouth
your verbal axé
restoring to me the language
that was mine
and was stolen from me
blow Eshu your breath
to the bottom of my throat
down where the voicebud
sprouts so the
bud may blossom
blooming into the flower of
my ancient speech
returned to me by your power
mount me on the axé of words
pregnant with your dynamic grounding
and I shall ride Orun's
supernatural infinity
roam the distances
of our Aiyê made of
uncertain dangerous land.

—Abdias do Nascimento
From Orixás

Well taught is the doctrine:
Lead a holy life for the extinction of suffering.

—TEACHING ASCRIBED TO THE BUDDHA

During the picking season my grandmother would get out of bed at four o'clock (she never used an alarm clock) and creak down to her knees and chant in a sleep-filled voice, "Our Father, thank you for letting me see this New Day. Thank you that you didn't allow the bed I lay on last night be my cooling board, nor my blanket my winding sheet. Guide my feet this day along the straight and narrow, and help me to put a bridle on my tongue. Bless this house and everybody in it. Thank you, in the name of your son, Jesus Christ, Amen."

—Maya Angelou
From *I Know Why the Caged Bird Sings*

Antibon-Legba, remove the barrier for me, Agwé!
Papa Legba remove the barrier
So I may pass through
When I come back I will salute the loa
Vodou Legba, remove the barrier for me
So that I may come back;
When I come back I will thank loa, Abobo.

—Haitian Vodou Prayer

They had entered this church, these doors; and
when the pastor made the altar call, she rose,
while she heard them praising God, and walked
down the long church aisle; down this aisle, to
this altar, before this golden cross; to these tears,
into this battle—would the battle end one day?

—James Baldwin
From Go Tell It on the Mountain

Gilberto Wilson

In the midst of sorrow or joy, sickness or health, adversity or prosperity, grant, we beseech Thee, that we may never lose sight of Thee. And when the storms of confusion and uncertainty overtake us, speak peace to our soul, O blessed Lord, and enlighten our mind with Thy Holy Spirit. Lighten our burdens by strengthening our spirit. Keep us strong and give us courage.

—JESSE JAI McNEIL
"WE CAST OURSELVES UPON THEE"

HE IS RISEN

STAN SHERER

Then turning to the disciples He [Jesus] said privately, "Blessed are the eyes which see what you see! For I tell you that many prophets and kings desired to see what you see, and did not see it, and to hear what you hear, and did not hear it."

—LUKE 10:23–24

The God who created the sun which gives us light, who rouses the waves and rules the storm, though hidden in the clouds, he watches us. He sees all what the white man does. The God of the white man inspires him to crime, but our God calls upon us to do good works. Our God who is good to us orders us to revenge our wrongs. He will direct our arms and aid us. Throw away the symbols of the God of the whites who has often caused us to weep, and listen to the voice of liberty, which speaks in the hearts of us all.

—Prayer attributed to Boukman, a leader of the Haitian Revolution, 1791

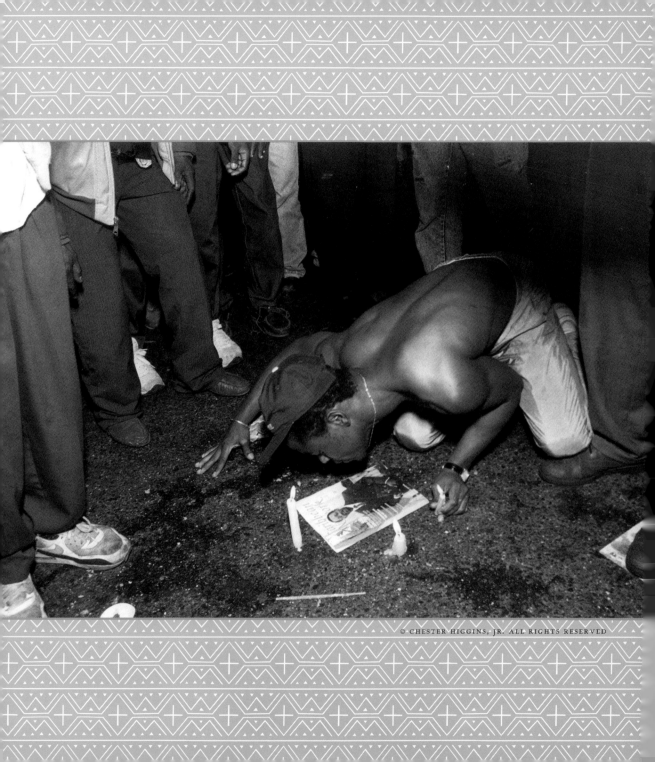

Say: "Allah's guidance is the (only) guidance, and we have been directed to submit ourselves to the Lord of the worlds; To establish regular prayers and to fear Allah: for it is to Him that we shall be gathered together."

—Qur'ân, Chapter 6: 71–72

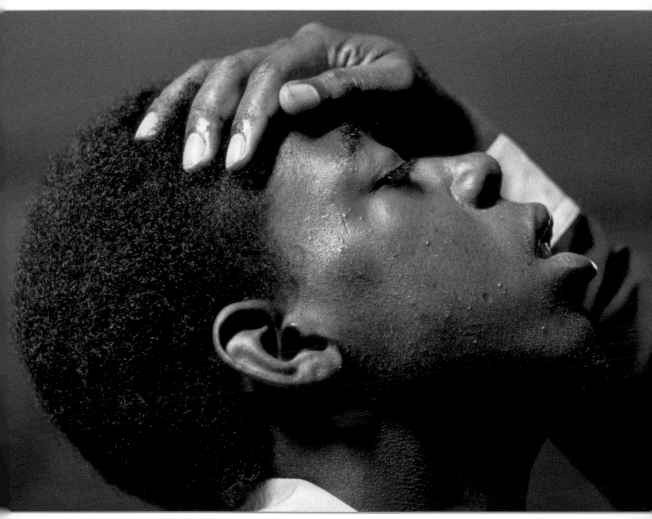

MARK PETERSON

Plenty of times you sent help my way, but i hid
and I remember once you held me close, but i slid
There was something that I just had to see
that you wanted me to see so I can be what you wanted me to be
And I think I've seen it, but I don't feel the same
Matter of fact I know I've seen it, I can feel the change
and it's strange almost got me beating down your door
But I have never known a love like this before
It's a wonderful feeling to get away from the pain
and up under the ceiling I get away from the rain
And the strain that I feel when I'm here is gone
I know real so I wipe away the tears with a song

—DMX

"Prayer (Skit)," from It's Dark and Hell Is Hot

DORIS ULMANN

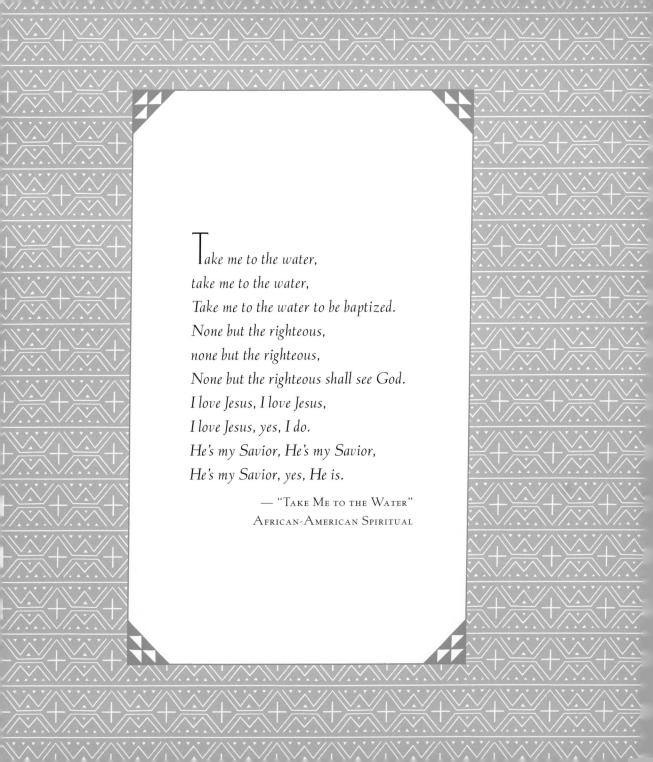

Take me to the water,
take me to the water,
Take me to the water to be baptized.
None but the righteous,
none but the righteous,
None but the righteous shall see God.
I love Jesus, I love Jesus,
I love Jesus, yes, I do.
He's my Savior, He's my Savior,
He's my Savior, yes, He is.

— "Take Me to the Water"
African-American Spiritual

What a fellowship, what a joy divine,
Leaning on the everlasting arms;
What a blessedness, what a peace is mine,
Leaning on the everlasting arms.
Leaning, leaning,
Leaning on Jesus Christ, my Savior,
Safe and secure from all alarms;
Leaning on the everlasting arms.

—Elisha A. Hoffman
"Leaning on the Everlasting Arms," 1887

May he support us all the day long,
till the shadows lengthen
and the evening comes
and the busy world is hushed
and the fever of life is over
and our work is done—
then in his mercy—
may he give us a safe lodging
and a holy rest
and peace at the last.

—ATTRIBUTED TO JOHN HENRY NEWMAN
"AND PEACE AT LAST"

This world is one great battlefield,
With forces all arrayed;
If in my heart I do not yield,
I'll overcome some day.
I'll overcome some day,
I'll overcome some day;
If in my heart
I do not yield
I'll overcome some day.

—Charles A. Tindley
"I'll Overcome Someday"

My way may not be easy
You did not say that it would be.
But if it gets dark,
I can't see my way,
You told me to put my trust in Thee,
that's why I'm asking You.
Lord, help me to hold out,
Lord, help me to hold out,
Lord, help me to hold out
until my change comes. . . .
I believe that I can hold out!
I believe that I can hold out!
I believe that I can hold out!
until my change comes.

—JAMES CLEVELAND
"LORD, HELP ME TO HOLD OUT"

To Allah belongs whatever is in the heavens and whatever is in the earth, and whether you reveal that which is in your minds or conceal it Allah will call you to account according to it. Then He will protect whomsoever He will and will punish whomsoever He will. And Allah is Possessor of full power to do all He will.

—Qur'ân, Chapter 2:284

ROLAND CHARLES FINE ART COLLECTION, COURTESY DEBORAH CHARLES

We come in great faith that
In your word you did say, "Ask,
And it shall be given,
Seek, and ye shall find, knock,
And the door will be open."
We ask in the precious name
Of Jesus that you would grant
Us Healing of the mind,
That we might glorify and
Give witness to the unlimited
Love and Blessings received
Each day of our lives.
We thank you, dear Father, we know
That you can and we know
That you will.

—Reverend Lillie Kate Benitez
"Prayer of Healing"

Our Father and Our God,
We come now to ask that your healing power
Will come upon all of these thy children.
Whatever the problem is, Heavenly Father, we pray
that you will answer it: where there's sickness—we pray
That you will bring about health; where there's loneliness—
     we pray that you will bring comfort; where there is hate—
     we pray that you usher in love.
We need you this morning, Heavenly Father. We want
     you to come by this church. Fill us with joy divine
     and reverence and make a home here with us.

—FRANK L. HORTON
"OUR FATHER AND OUR GOD"

STEVE HART

117

In a culture filled with divisiveness, disconnectedness and domination, we pause for a moment of centered-cosmic Christian connection that will bring wholeness and healing to ourselves and our world. O God, liberate us from the domination of individual and institutional violence. Liberate us for the ministry of deliverance to the captives within and without. Liberate us from a self-centered spiritual materialism and liberate us to serve the present age. Liberate us from building our kingdoms and liberate us for the Kingdom of God.

—FRANK MADISON REID III
"A PRAYER FOR LIBERATION
THAT LEADS TO LIBERATING LOVE"

Lord, it's more than I'll ever understand,
how I am preserved by thy hand.
But then there's only
two things required of me:
to be faithful (because I've been set free)
and to be willing to be used by Thee.
So Lord I come willing to be used by Thee.

—GENNA RAE MCNEIL
"LORD, I'M WILLING"

How darkness seemed to gather around me,
and in my desperation I looked up and said,
"O Lord, I have come down here to die, and I must
have salvation this afternoon or death.
If you send me to hell I will go, but convert my soul."

—AMANDA BERRY SMITH
FROM AN AUTOBIOGRAPHY:
THE STORY OF THE LORD'S DEALINGS
WITH MRS. AMANDA SMITH,
THE COLORED EVANGELIST

Make speed, O Lord, to build me into a fortress for the Holy Spirit, Raise me up lest I crumble into a desolate ruin of sin. Make speed to forgive for forgiveness is with thee.

O Lord, thou knowest the balm to heal my wounds, the help to strengthen my weakness, the path to prosper my progress. Thou knowest all that is expedient to fulfil my life, as the potter knows how to contrive his own vessel's perfection. For the work is wrought according to the design and wisdom of its maker.

O Lord, renew thy vessel with the power of the Holy Spirit. Make the work of thy hands to be lovely and indestructible.

—"Hymn to the Blessed Virgin"
Ethiopian Orthodox Prayer

125

And He [Allah] will teach him the Book
and the Wisdom, and the Torah and the Gospel.

—QUR'ÂN, CHAPTER 3:47

O Lord our God, thou alone art holy, who hast bestowed thy holy things on all of us by thy invisible power.

Yea Lord, we pray thee and beseech thee to send the Holy Spirit upon this church and this ark and upon all the holy vessels whereon thy precious mystery will be celebrated.

And now, bless them, sanctify them, purify them from all uncleanness and stain through the forgiveness of the second birth that they may be free for ever from the least remembrance of defilement and uncleanness.

And make this church and this ark vessels chosen and clean and pure, refined seven times from all spot and stain and uncleanness or transgressors like the cleansing of silver from earth, refined and purified and tested.

And grant that on them when they are clean and holy be performed the Sacrament of the Father and the Son and the Holy Spirit, both now and ever and world without end. Amen.

—Prayer for Church Sanctification
Ethiopian Orthodox Tradition

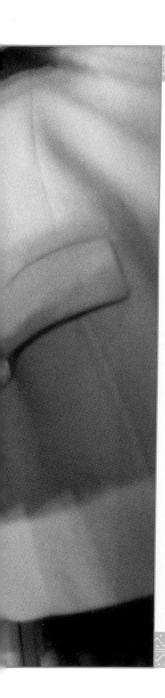

Lord, sustain us, lead us, and guide us and when we get low,
lift us and when we get wrong, correct us.
And when we go out on the deep end, give us a life raft
to bring us back to the shore. But Lord, be with us and stand by us and your name which is worthy shall have all the praise,
for we ask these blessings in the name of the One
whose Kingdom shall have no end.
Amen.

—James A. Forbes, Jr.

STAN SHERER

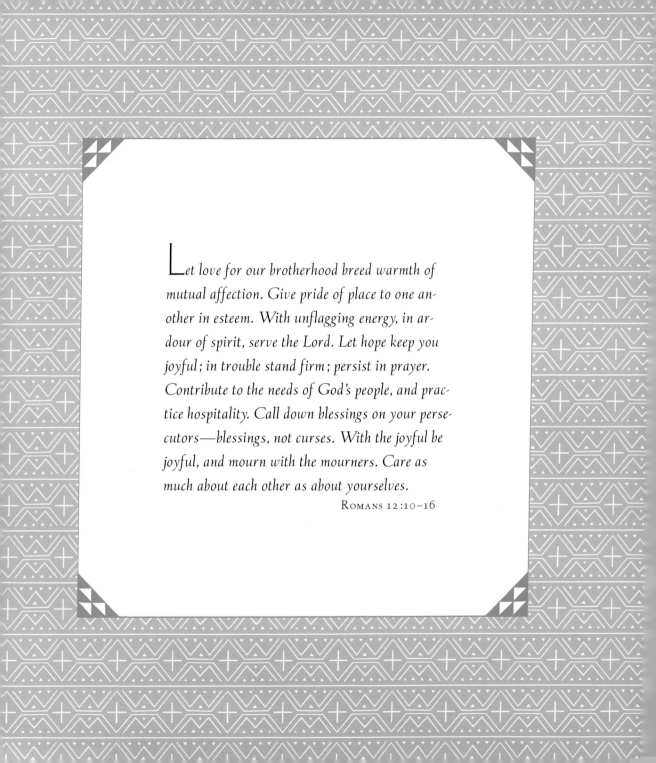

Let love for our brotherhood breed warmth of mutual affection. Give pride of place to one another in esteem. With unflagging energy, in ardour of spirit, serve the Lord. Let hope keep you joyful; in trouble stand firm; persist in prayer. Contribute to the needs of God's people, and practice hospitality. Call down blessings on your persecutors—blessings, not curses. With the joyful be joyful, and mourn with the mourners. Care as much about each other as about yourselves.

ROMANS 12:10–16

May all beings everywhere plagued
with sufferings of body and mind
quickly be freed from their illnesses.

May those frightened cease to be afraid,
and may those bound be free.

May the powerless find power,
and may people think of befriending
one another.

May those who find themselves in trackless,
fearful wilderness—the children, the aged, the unprotected—
be guarded by beneficial celestials,
and may they swiftly attain Buddhahood (enlightenment).

—Buddhist salutation for peace

134

Princes shall come out of Egypt,
Ethiopia shall stretch forth her
hand unto God. Oh thou God
of Ethiopia, thou God of divine
majesty, thy spirit come within our
hearts to dwell in the parts of righteousness. That the hungry be fed,
the sick nourished, the aged protected,
and the infant cared for. Teach us
love and loyalty as it is in Zion.

—A RASTAFARIAN PRAYER

OMOBOWALE AYORINDE

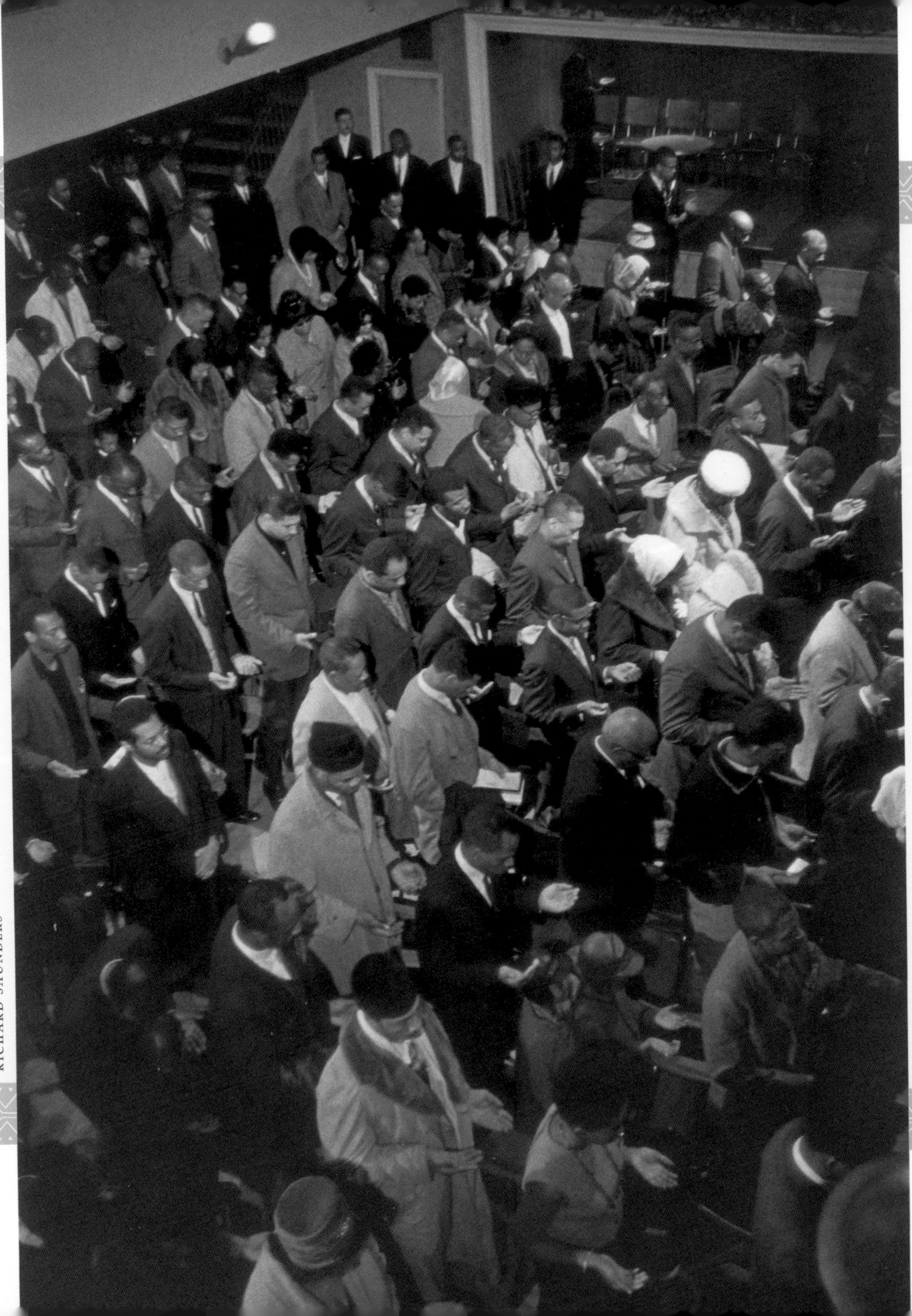

RICHARD SAUNDERS

Our Lord! we have heard the call of
one calling (us) to Faith, "Believe ye in the
Lord," and we have believed. Our Lord!
Forgive us our sins, blot out from us our
inequities, and take to Thyself our souls
in the company of the righteous.

—Qur'ân, Chapter 3: 193

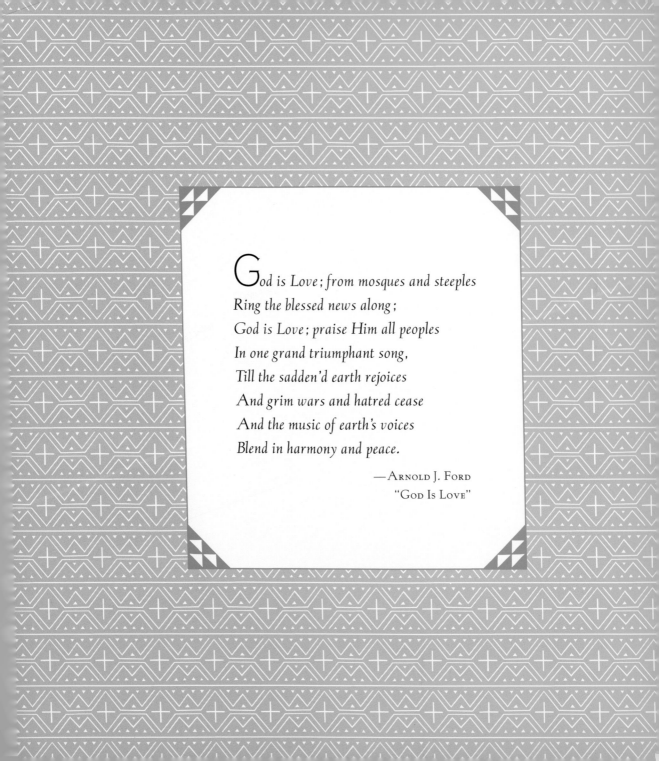

God is Love; from mosques and steeples
Ring the blessed news along;
God is Love; praise Him all peoples
In one grand triumphant song,
Till the sadden'd earth rejoices
And grim wars and hatred cease
And the music of earth's voices
Blend in harmony and peace.

—Arnold J. Ford
"God Is Love"

P lease close this war which is very mean
Teach us how to live together again.
You are the greatest general, you are the greatest dean.
Forgive and blot out our sins.
Smile on the soil, touch it with your blood.
In Jesus' name I pray.

—Elizabeth J. Dabney
"O My God, Please Close This War"

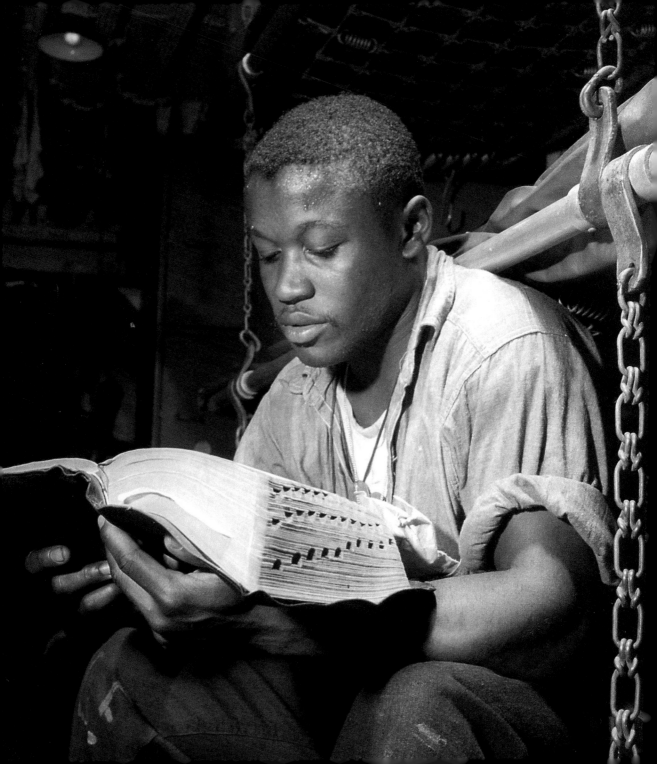

GILBERTO WILSON

Oh yes, fix me, Jesus, fix me.
Fix me so that I can walk on
a little while longer.
Fix me so that I can pray on
just a little bit harder.
Fix me so that I can sing on
just a little bit louder.
Fix me so that I can go on despite the pain,
the fear, the doubt, and, yes, the anger.
I ask not that you take this cross from me,
only that you give me the strength to continue carrying it onward
'til my dying day.
Oh, fix me, Jesus, fix me.

—"FIX ME, JESUS, FIX ME"
AFRICAN-AMERICAN SPIRITUAL

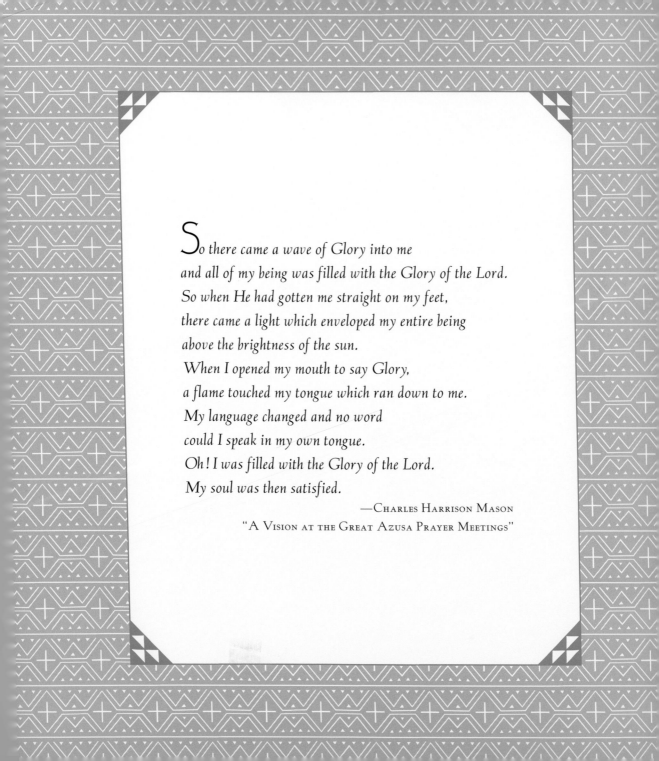

So there came a wave of Glory into me
and all of my being was filled with the Glory of the Lord.
So when He had gotten me straight on my feet,
there came a light which enveloped my entire being
above the brightness of the sun.
When I opened my mouth to say Glory,
a flame touched my tongue which ran down to me.
My language changed and no word
could I speak in my own tongue.
Oh! I was filled with the Glory of the Lord.
My soul was then satisfied.

—CHARLES HARRISON MASON
"A VISION AT THE GREAT AZUSA PRAYER MEETINGS"

GILBERTO WILSON

May it be Your will, HaShem,
that You renew for us
a good and sweet year.

—A PRAYER FOR ROSH HASHANAH,
THE JEWISH NEW YEAR

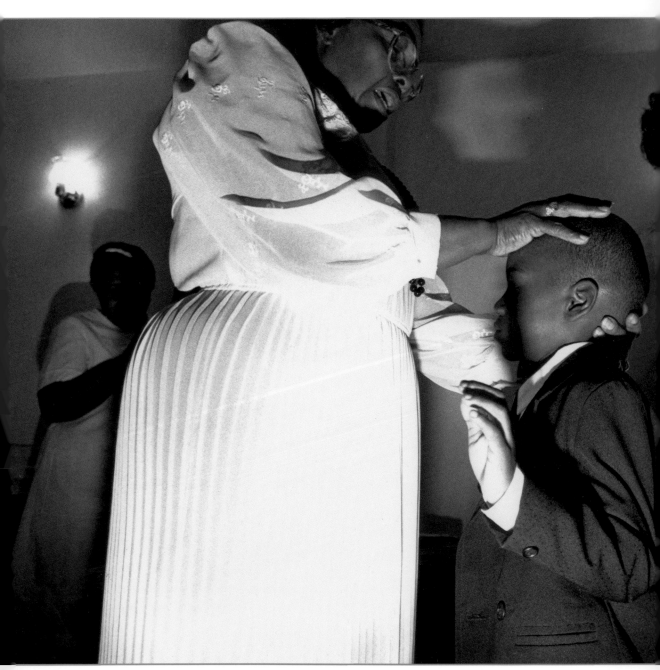

STEVE HART

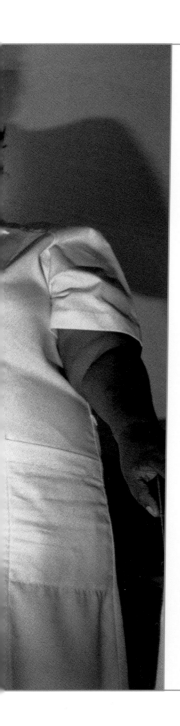

My faith looks up to Thee,
Thou Lamb of Calvary, Savior divine!
Now hear me while I pray,
Take all my guilt away,
O let me from this day
Be wholly Thine!

—Ray Palmer
"My Faith Looks Up to Thee"

T he Lord our God, the Lord is one!
You shall love the Lord your God with all your
heart, with all your soul, and with all your
strength. And these words which I command
you today shall be in your heart. You shall
teach them diligently to your children, and shall
talk of them when you sit in your house, when
you walk by the way, when you lie down, and
when you rise up.

—Deuteronomy 6: 5–7

God, if You are there,
I need You to reveal Yourself to me.

—WELLINGTON BOONE
FROM *BREAKING THROUGH*

ASSOCIATED PRESS, AP

Verily We have granted thee a manifest victory:
That Allah may forgive thee thy faults of the past
and those to follow; fulfil His favour to
thee; and guide thee on the Straight Way;
And that Allah may help thee with powerful help.

—Qur'ân, Chapter 48: 1–3

MOIRA PERNAMBUCO

And we know that there is a God
somewhere in the marvelous, magnificent and miracle-making name
    that brings healing in the midst of our sickness,
that brings joy in the midst of our sorrow,
that brings strength even for those who are downtrodden
and who makes a way out of no way.
We give thanks right now
in the power of the spirit of the living God.

—James Melvin Washington
From the Schomburg Center's
"Invoking the Spirit" Exhibition Forum

Come to the altar. Just leave your burdens there. Somebody's home is torn up tonight. You scuffling mothers with your fatherless children. I raised mine by myself. I know what a scuffle is when mothers have to pretend they are full so the child could get the food. I know what you're going through. Come on women. Come on mothers. Let's take this thing to God. These men have walked out on us and left us holding the bag. We've made mistakes but God has forgiven us. Let's get it straight. . . . No talking or walking. Souls are at stake here. Praise our God.

—FROM BELIEF, RITUAL, AND PERFORMANCE IN A BLACK PENTECOSTAL CHURCH BY THOMASINA NEELY

Great God of justice,
grant that the dark night of injustice will give
      way to the dawning of a brighter day.
      Give thy people respite from the heat
      of constant battle. But never let us give
      up until the victory is won.
Forgive us our complacency,
for we will do better, or we will die.
Help us to always protest against evil.
But also give us the strength to produce the good.
      In the Name of the Name
about every name.
Amen.

—REVEREND DR. MACK KING CARTER
"A PRAYER AGAINST INJUSTICE"

163

O Lord, the hard-won miles
Have worn my stumbling feet:
Oh, soothe me with thy smiles,
And make my life complete.

The thorns were thick and keen
Where'er I trembling trod;
The way was long between
My wounded feet and God.

Where healing waters flow
Do thou my footsteps lead.
My heart is aching so;
Thy gracious balm I need.

—PAUL LAURENCE DUNBAR
"A PRAYER"

STEVE HART

Can a mother forget her child? Can a woman forget the fruit of her womb? Even if these forget, I will never forget you. See, upon the palms of my hands I have written your name.

—ISAIAH 49: 15–16

Saint Anne
The De Beaupre

AUSTIN HANSEN

Scattered by earth's many waters,
Pilgrims searching for the Light,
Ethiopia's sons and daughters
At thy throne, O God, unite
Keep us ever close together,
One with heart and aim to fight.

One to praise with pride and gladness
The Great hand which fix'd our race
One to share each other's sadness,
One to trust Thy saving grace
And forgiving, sweetly living
Till with joy we see Thy face.

Thou, who didst from Pharaoh's raving
Israel's sons and daughters free,
Free us from the sin of craving
Other than Thou wouldst us be;
But t'aspire raise us higher
Till we reach our goal in Thee.

—ARNOLD J. FORD
"AFRICA"

I want Jesus to walk with me,
I want Jesus to walk with me,
All along my pilgrim journey,
Lord, I want Jesus to walk with me.

In my trials, Lord, walk with me,
In my trials, Lord, walk with me,
When the shades of life are falling,
Lord, I want Jesus to walk with me.

—"I WANT JESUS TO WALK WITH ME"
AFRICAN-AMERICAN SPIRITUAL

When the storms of life are raging,
Stand by me;
When the storms of life are raging,
Stand by me.
When the world is tossing me,
Like a ship upon the sea;
Thou who rulest wind and water,
Stand by me.

—CHARLES ALBERT TINDLEY
"STAND BY ME"

My soul is being healed. I'm bathing in Him. When He comes He removes the hurt, the bitterness, the soreness. He removes the tiredness. He heals the body. He eases the mind. He comforts the soul. Thank you, Jesus. He's here. Thank God for the Lamb. Thank God for the Lamb.

—From Belief, Ritual, and Performance in a Black Pentecostal Church by Thomasina Neely

STEVE HART

Master Tranca-Ruas

It is said that your people belong to the Faith

And we, your devout worshippers say

That your band is the greatest!

Master Tranca-Ruas

We begin the Congo ritual of song and dance

Long live the Faith of Guinea!

Long live the Souls!

Long live the Kingdom of the Faith!

Long live Exu of the Souls!

For he is Tranca-Ruas of the Faith.

Mama is begging the sun

Papa is begging the moon

Your children are begging

The protection of Master Tranca-Ruas!

—"Exu Who Locks Up the Streets"

Jesus has sailed to your shore—through the storms—to climb the rocky hills of trouble in your life. Though the world seems against you, though friends and family seem to cast you aside, he stands ready and waiting to unshackle your soul and let you taste heaven's joy of salvation. Unshackled . . . from death! Unshackled . . . from the grave! Unshackled . . . from the power of sin! Unshackled . . . to tell the Good News!

—Paige L. Chargois
"Unshackled!"

Hail Mary, full of grace,
the Lord is with thee,
blessed art thou among women,
and blessed is the fruit of thy womb, Jesus.

Holy Mary, Mother of God,
pray for us sinners,
now and at the hour of our death.
Amen

—"Hail Mary"

AUSTIN HANSEN

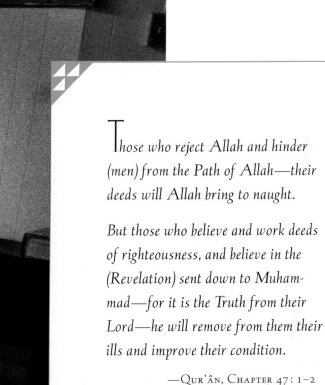

Those who reject Allah and hinder
(men) from the Path of Allah—their
deeds will Allah bring to naught.

But those who believe and work deeds
of righteousness, and believe in the
(Revelation) sent down to Muham-
mad—for it is the Truth from their
Lord—he will remove from them their
ills and improve their condition.

—Qur'ân, Chapter 47: 1–2

Lord, in this thy mercy's day,
ere for us it pass away,
on our knees we fall and pray.

Holy Jesus, grant us tears,
fill us with heart-searching fears,
ere that awful doom appear.

Lord, on us thy Spirit pour,
kneeling lowly at thy door,
ere it close forevermore.

—Isaac Williams
"Lord, in This Thy Mercy's Day"

HAROLD E. RHYNIE

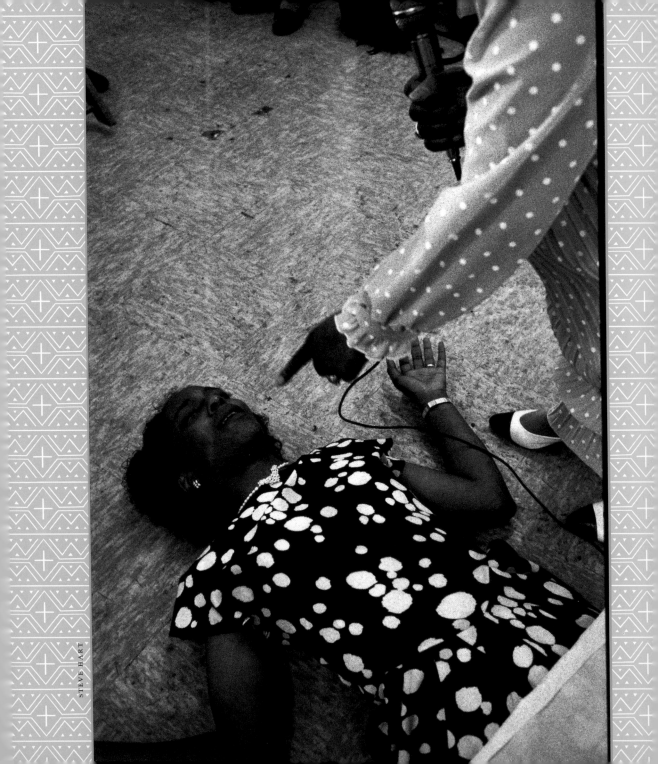

Blessed is the man [or woman] whom God corrects;
So do not despise the discipline of the Almighty.
For He wounds, but He also binds up;
He injures, but His hands also heal.
From six calamities He will rescue you;
In seven no harm will befall you.
In famine He will ransom you from death,
And in battle from the stroke of the sword.
You will be protected from the lash of the tongue,
And need not fear when destruction comes.

—JOB 5:17–21

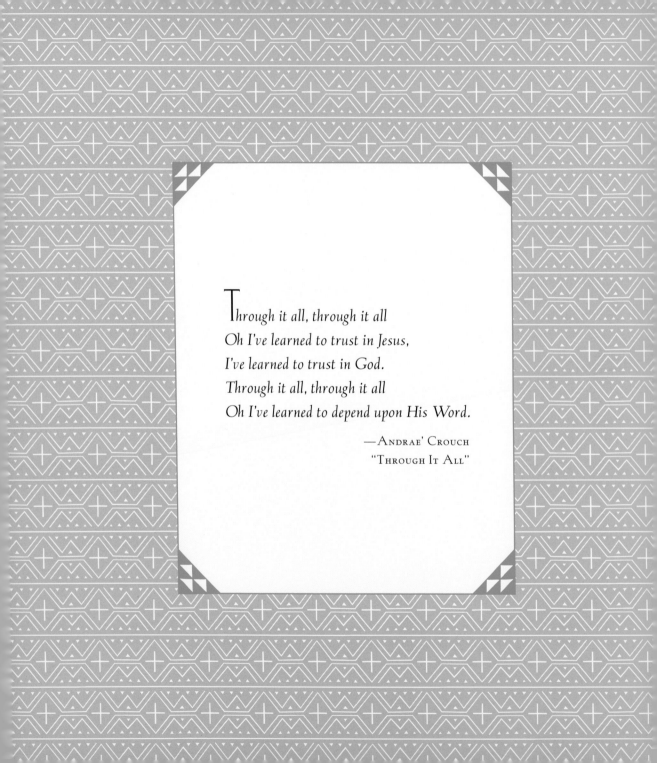

Through it all, through it all
Oh I've learned to trust in Jesus,
I've learned to trust in God.
Through it all, through it all
Oh I've learned to depend upon His Word.

—ANDRAE' CROUCH
"THROUGH IT ALL"

GILBERTO WILSON

This is the call to discipleship. I want to pray for somebody who wants to be saved tonight. I want you to step out in the aisle right here right quick. I want to pray for you. Somebody wants to rededicate their lives to God. I'm not going to wait all night. You know whether or not you want this prayer. Come now. . . . But I want to pray. Somebody in our midst tonight came. You're not saved and we don't want to embarrass. God bless those that are coming. They're coming. They're coming. Thank you, Lord.

—From *Belief, Ritual, and Performance in a Black Pentecostal Church* by Thomasina Neely

GILBERTO WILSON

I Am *renewed, authorized and cleansed by the authority*
of the Holy Spirit within me.
My steps are ordered, guided and blessed.
I Am *a worthy vessel.*
I Am *a willing vessel.*
I have been shaped and modeled by God's love.
I Am *available for God's love*
to be accomplished as me.
I Am *equipped with the skill, the knowledge and the ability to carry*
out the life assignments that God has given to me with love.
I now go forth peacefully, joyfully and lovingly.
I Am *bestowed with an abundance of good things in all*
of my affairs and in every aspect of my world.

—Iyanla Vanzant
"I Am!"

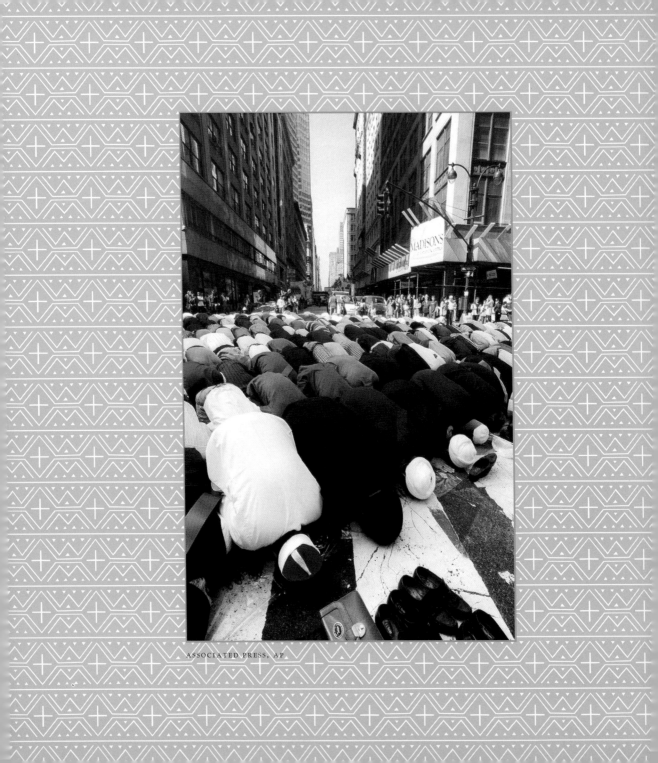

And between the two (the Fire and the Paradise) is a barrier, and on the elevated places there shall be men (like the Prophets and other exalted spiritual dignitaries) who will recognize everyone by his appearance. And they shall call out to the (prospective) inmates of Paradise, "Peace be on you!" These (prospective inmates of Paradise) will not have (yet) entered therein, though they will be hoping (for this entry). And when their eyes are turned towards the fellows of the Fire, they will say, "Our Lord! Place us not with these wrong-doing people."

—Qu'rân, Chapter 7: 46–47

All Mighty and all wise God our Heavenly Father,
tis once more and again that a few of Your beloved children
are gathered together to call upon Your Holy Name.
We bow at Your footstool of mercy Master to thank
you for our spared lives. We thank You that we are
able to get up this morning clothed in our right mind.
For Master, since we met here many have been snatched
out of the land of the living and hurled into eternity.
But through Your goodness and mercy we have been
spared to assemble ourselves here once more to call
upon a captain who has never lost a battle.

—MELVA W. COSTEN
FROM THE SCHOMBURG CENTER'S
"INVOKING THE SPIRIT" EXHIBITION FORUM

STEVE HART

REV. MARTIN LUTHER KING. JR.

1929 — 1968

"Free at last. Free at last.
Thank God Almighty
I'm Free at last.

TAMI CHAPPELL/REUTERS

We thank thee, O God, for the spiritual nature of man.
We are in nature but we live above nature.
Help us never to let anybody or
any condition pull us so low as to cause us to hate.
Give us strength to love our enemies and to do good
to those who despitefully use us and persecute us.
We thank thee for thy Church,
founded upon thy Word, that challenges us to do more
than sing and pray, but go out and work as though
the very answer to our prayers depended on us and not upon thee.
Then, finally, help us to realize that man was created
to shine like stars and live on through all eternity.
Keep us, we pray, in perfect peace;
help us to walk together, pray together, sing together,
and live together until that day when all God's children,
Black, White, Red, and Yellow will rejoice
in one common bond of humanity in the kingdom
of our Lord and of our God, we pray.
Amen.

—Reverend Dr. Martin Luther King, Jr.
"A Pastoral Prayer"

For we wrestle not against flesh and blood, but against principalities, against powers, against the rulers of the darkness of this world, against spiritual wickedness in high places.

Wherefore take unto you the whole armour of God, that ye may be able to withstand in the evil day, and having done all, to stand.

Stand therefore, having your loins girt about with truth, and having on the breastplate of righteousness; And your feet shod with the preparation of the gospel of peace;

Above all, taking the shield of faith, wherewith ye shall be able to quench all the fiery darts of the wicked. And take the helmet of salvation, and the sword of the Spirit, which is the word of God.

—Ephesians 6:12–17

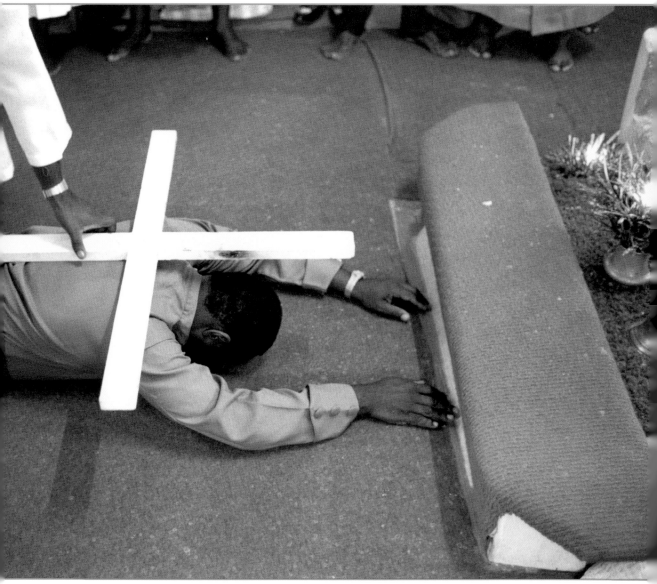

And then, dear Lord, keep watch with those
who work or watch or weep this night.
And give your angels charge over those who sleep
and tend the sick, Lord Christ.
Give rest to the weary. Bless the dying. Soothe the suffering.
Pity the afflicted. Shield the joyous.
And do it all, God, because You love us.
And we will be careful to give You all the praise and the
    glory because we know that Your will will be done.
Amen.

—Canon Frederick B. Williams
From the Schomburg Center's
"Invoking the Spirit" Exhibition Forum

O Thou light of the world, shine in upon our darkness and illumine the truth that all men may see it. For men are more ignorant than wicked— willfully ignorant it is true and wickedly willful— and yet it is because the world does not know and realize the truth about itself and about its human children that it is continually doing such monstrous and hurtful things. Give us then light, more light, O God, that we may see and learn and know and we may no longer be with them that sit in darkness.

—Inspired by John 8:12–16
From Prayers for Dark People by W. E. B. Du Bois

ASSOCIATED PRESS, AP

In those times of our feeling overwhelmed, speak to us, Lord. Help us remember that we do not travel distance all at one time, but step by step, day by day, hour by hour, and minute by minute and that we walk by faith, not by sight.

As we face what is ahead, give to us a sense of priority and proper ordering so that we will keep the responsibilities of life and our own strength and abilities in proper focus.

—WILLIAM D. WATLEY
"I GROW WEARY"

*S*weet spirit, grant us the faith to resist our resistance to Thee. Oh God, God, I pray that you will bless us with a mighty increase in the gift of prayer amongst our people and in every culture, other culture, race, and nation on this abused planet. Liberate us for service in the ministries of word, deed, and sacrament. May we rediscover our oneness in the unyielding, yet often belittled fact of our own diversity, indeed the diversity of creation itself.

—James Melvin Washington
From the Schomburg Center's
"Invoking the Spirit" exhibition forum

To Him belongs the keys of the heavens and the earth: He enlarges and restricts the Sustenance to whom He will: for He knows full well all things.

The same religion has He established for you as that which He enjoined on Noah—that which We have sent by inspiration to thee—and that which We enjoined on Abraham, Moses, and Jesus: namely, that ye should remain steadfast in Religion, and make no divisions therein: to those who worship other things than Allah, hard is the (way) to which thou callest them. Allah chooses to Himself those whom He pleases, and guides to Himself those who turn (to Him).

—Qur'ân, Chapter 42: 12–13

The Lord is my pace-setter, I shall not rush.

He makes me stop and rest for quiet intervals;

He provides me with images of stillness,

which restore my serenity.

He leads me in ways of efficiency through calmness of mind.

And His guidance is peace.

Even though I have a great many things to accomplish each day,

I will not fret, for His presence is here.

His timelessness, his all-importance will keep me in balance.

He prepares refreshment and renewal in the midst of my activity

By anointing my mind with His oils of tranquility.

My cup of joyous energy overflows.

Surely harmony and effectiveness shall be the fruit of my hours for

I shall walk in the place of my Lord and dwell in His House forever.

—ALL SAINTS CONVENT, CANTONVILLE, MARYLAND
"THE NUNS' TWENTY-THIRD PSALM"

DIXIE D. VEREEN

C ome and go with me to my Father's house,
To my Father's house, to my Father's house.
Come and go with me to my Father's house,
There is joy, joy, joy.

There's peace and happiness there in my Father's house,
In my Father's house, in my Father's house.
There's peace and happiness there in my Father's house,
There is joy, joy, joy.

—Traditional Hymn

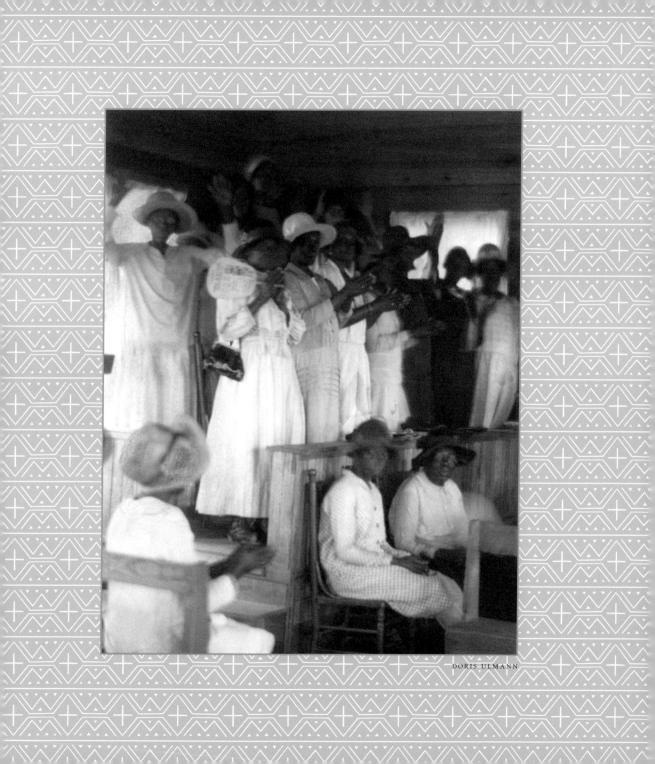

DORIS ULMANN

Oh God! Receive the morning greetings!
Ancestors! Receive the morning greetings!
We are here on the chosen day,
We are going to sow the seed,
We are going out to cultivate.
Oh God! Cause the millet to germinate,
Make the eight seeds sprout,
And the ninth calabash.

Give a wife to him who has none!
And to him who has a wife without children
Give a child!
Protect the men against thorns,
Against snake-bites,
Against ill winds!

Pour out the rain,
As we pour water from a pot!
Millet! Come!

—A Dogon Greeting to God at Sowing Time

Lord, I am happy this morning.
Birds and angels sing and I am exultant.
The universe and our hearts are open to your grace.
I feel my body and give thanks.
The sun burns my skin and I thank you.
The breakers are rolling toward the seashore,
The sea foam splashes our house.
I give thanks.

Lord, I rejoice in your creation,
and that you are behind it, and before,
and next to it, and above—and within us.

—"My Joys Mount as Do the Birds"
Ghana

NOTES ON PHOTOGRAPHS AND PRAYERS

The biblical passages in *Standing in the Need of Prayer* were drawn from the following bibles: New American Bible, Revised Standard Version, New King James Version, New Jerusalem Bible, New International Version, and The Living Bible. Koranic sources are The Holy Qur'ân (English translation by Amatul Rahmân Omar and Abdul Mannân Omar) and The Holy Qur'ân (English translation by Abdullah Yusuf Ali).

(Page 9)

From the photographer's church series, ca. 1956–1963.

(Page 11)

The late Reverend Steve Griffin, former pastor of Little Zion Baptist Church, raises his hand to baptize a young girl in the church's baptismal pool located under the pulpit, Marrero, Louisiana, 1973. All those formally converting to Christianity are required to be baptized as a condition for joining the church. This sacrament symbolizes the washing away of the old life and the adoption of a life defined by Christian values.

(Page 12)

From the photographer's church series, ca. 1956–1963.

(Page 14)

Religious pilgrim reading bible and meditation, Lalibela, Ethiopia, 1985.
The Ethiopian Orthodox Church traces its history to the fourth century, A.D.
The denomination calls itself *Tewahedo*, meaning union.

(Page 17)

From the photographer's storefront church series, ca. 1987. Dating back at least
to eighteenth-century outdoor tent and prayer meetings, storefront churches or
nontraditional church edifices of a variety of religions and denominations are common in
the African-American religious experience.

(Page 18)

Muslim woman at prayer, Savior's Day gathering, Nation of Islam, Chicago, Illinois, 1966.

(Page 21)

From the photographer's Brooklyn Word Church series, Brooklyn, New York, 1988–89.

(Page 23)

Old woman in prayer during the Ethiopian Christmas known as Genna, celebrated on January 7, Addis Ababa, Ethiopia, ca. 1985. A forty-day period of fasting leads up to Genna.

(Page 24)

Malcolm X, New York, New York, ca. 1963.
This Al-Fatihah prayer accompanying the photograph is transcribed from Malcolm X's
personal Qu'rân, which is now part of the Malcolm X Collection at the
Schomburg Center for Research in Black Culture. In January 2003 a large collection
of Malcolm X's diaries, photos, letters, and other materials were placed on
long-term deposit to the Schomburg Center by the Estate of Betty Shabazz.

(Page 26)

Nurses praying before going on duty, Ghana, 1967.

(Page 29)

From the photographer's Brooklyn Word Church series, Brooklyn, New York, 1988–89.

(Page 30)

Spiritual Baptist in Barbados, 1988.

Indigenous to Barbados and Trinidad, the Spiritual Baptist Church maintains
an African context and perspective to Christian doctrine, like the syncretistic
African-based religions of Brazil (Candomblé), Cuba (Santeria), and Haiti (Vodou).
Its theology includes a belief in the communication with God, or visitation of the
Holy Spirit, through visions, dreams, and prayer.

(Page 33)

Kneeling children with heads bowed in prayer, South Carolina, ca. 1929.

(Page 34)

From the photographer's Brooklyn Word Church series, Brooklyn, New York, 1988–89.

(Page 37)

From the photographer's Street Baptismal/Last Ritual in Harlem series,
New York, New York, 1987–98. The United House of Prayer for All People's
annual baptismal is held in the street with the congregation "submerged"
under the water from a fire hose that is blessed.

(Page 39)

Sunday service, Christ Temple United Baptist Church,
Brooklyn, New York, 1990.

(Page 40)

Young man dressed to receive Oxum, a female orixá
of the Candomblé religion, Bahia, Brazil, 1987.

Oxum, who is known as the goddess of love, is the youngest and most beautiful wife of Xangô, the lawgiver and god of war. Oxum's holy day is Saturday, and her greeting is "Oore Yèyé o!"—a Yoruba phrase meaning "The kindness of the Mother!"

Practitioners of Candomblé believe in one supreme being, known as Olodumaré, or Olurun, and a pantheon of deities, called orixás, who dwell in Orun, the spiritual realm of ancestors and spirits. Orixás may communicate, descend upon, or visit the living who reside in Aiyé or aye, the corporeal or physical world. Based primarily on Yoruban, Fon, and Bantu religious traditions, Candomblé regards both Orun and Aiyé as infused with the life force known as axé. Eshu, called the Trickster (also known as Elegba in Santeria and Legba in Vodou), is the messenger and mediator to the orixás.

(Page 42)

Among the oldest religions practiced in Africa, Judaism is observed by more than 200,000 African Americans today.

(Page 45)

Mourners hold a prayer meeting at the train station in Meridian, Mississippi, around the casket bearing the body of slain integration leader Medgar Evers, 1963. The body was driven from Jackson to Meridian and placed on a train for Washington, D.C., and burial in Arlington National Cemetery.

"Free at Last" was invoked by Reverend Dr. Martin Luther King, Jr., at the 1963 March on Washington. The opening words are inscribed on King's tombstone in Atlanta.

(Page 46)

Eucharist at St. Patrick's Church, Roxbury, Massachusetts, 1988.

(Page 48)

From the photographer's Brooklyn Word Church series, Brooklyn, New York, 1988–89.

(Page 51)

The Reverend Joan A. King gives praise on a Sunday morning at Metropolitan A.M.E. Church in Washington, D.C., ca. 1990.

(Page 53)

Lotus Temple Priest, Brooklyn, New York, 1990.

Developed by Dr. Maulana Karenga, who conceptualized Kwanzaa, the Husia is "taken from two ancient Egyptian words which signify the two divine powers" by which Ra created the world. *Hu*, meaning *authoritative utterance*, and *Sia*, meaning *exceptional insight*, are combined to express the divine character of an ancient African theology.

(Page 55)

Baptism, Abyssinian Baptist Church, New York, New York, 1998.

(Page 56)

The ordination of deacons with their wives inducted as deaconesses,
Abyssinian Baptist Church, New York, New York, 1999.

(Page 59)

Black and white students at Seaton Elementary School join in a prayer as public schools open on a non-segregated basis for the first time, Washington, D.C., 1954.

(Page 61)

Woman prays at September 11 memorial service in Miami at GESU Catholic Church at National Day of Prayer, September 14, 2001. Prayer services were held throughout the world in reaction to a coordinated terrorist attack on the World Trade Center and the Pentagon.

(Page 62)

Bethune-Cookman College choir sings The Lord's Prayer as Dr. Mary McLeod Bethune listens, bowing her head, during Sunday chapel services, Daytona Beach, Florida, 1943.

Gordon Parks, photographer, Library of Congress, Prints & Photographs Division, reproduction number LC-USW3-014845-C

(Page 65)

Members of congregation praying, St. Paul's Missionary Baptist Church, Valley View, Mississippi, 1964.

(Page 66)

Participants pause for a moment of prayer during the historic Selma to Montgomery march in March 1965. Five months later President Lyndon Johnson signed the Voting Rights Act of 1965.

(Page 69)

Boa Morte, Brazil, 1990. Founded in the eighteenth century, the Sisterhood of the Good Death (Irmandade da Boa Morte) is a Catholic Sisterhood formed during the days of enslavement in Bahia. Its members used Catholicism to camouflage their practice of Candomblé, a Yoruba-based religion. Members of this group, pooling their resources, were able to buy freedom for many enslaved Africans.

(Page 70)

Brother and sister saying their prayers, Greene County, Georgia, 1941.

Jack Delano, photographer, Library of Congress, Prints & Photographs Division, reproduction number LC-USF34-046523-D

(Page 73)

Muslim women in Harlem, New York, New York, 1985.

(Page 75)

Harlem Street Church, New York, New York, 1977.

(Page 76)

From the photographer's Brooklyn Word Church series, Brooklyn, New York, 1988–89.

(Page 78)

From the photographer's Brooklyn Word Church series, Brooklyn, New York, 1988–89.

(Page 81)

Reverend Clinton Miller, Dr. Calvin O. Butts III, Attorney Johnnie L. Cochran, Jr.,
and Reverend Kevin Johnson, New York, New York, 2000.
At Abyssinian Baptist Church, it is customary for the ministers to pray
in the pastor's office prior to the Sunday worship service.

(Page 82)

Prayers during ceremony giving presents to the oríxá Yemanja,
the deity of the sea, Brazil, 1990.

(Page 84)

Morning Gongyo (prayer), 2002. Soka Gakkai International (SGI-USA) members chant
"Nam Myoho Rerge Kyo" before the Gohonzon, an object of worship. The Gohonzon
serves as a "spiritual mirror," revealing the worshipper's own Buddha nature, the creative
essence of life. SGI-USA is an American Buddhist association.

(Page 87)

Evening prayer, Alabama, 1968.

(Page 89)

Purification ceremony to Agwé, the *loa* or spirit of the sea, Haiti, 1991.

In Vodou, Legba, often nicknamed the Trickster, serves as a spiritual intercessor, opening the way for deities or *loa* (lwa) to reach humans. To practitioners of Catholicism he is akin to St. Peter as a gatekeeper to heaven or St. Nicholas as protector or disciplinarian. It is believed that *loa* enter the body during songs and dances. Drumbeats bring together the heartbeats of the living and the *loa*.

(Page 90)

From the photographer's storefront church series, ca. 1987.

The altar call is a custom in Pentecostal and Evangelical churches to come forward to publicly "accept" Christ.

(Page 93)

Jefferson Baptist Church, Putnam County, Georgia, ca. 1940.

Courtesy National Archives, photo number 80-G-305241

235

(Page 94)

Visitation of the Holy Spirit, Spiritual Baptists in Barbados, 1988.

(Page 97)

Prayers during ceremony seeking support of a *loa* for
President Jean Bertrand Aristide, New York, New York, 1992.
In 1791 two leaders, Toussaint L'Ouverture and a man known as Boukman,
led the Haitian revolt against slavery. Boukman was killed in the conflict.

(Page 99)

More than 10,000 Muslims pray while celebrating Eid al-Adha, the Feast of Sacrifice,
Brooklyn, New York, 1999. The holiday is celebrated with prayers, small gifts for
children, distribution of food to the needy, and social gatherings.

Tent revival, St. Paul, Minnesota, 1984.

Two men standing in a river during baptism, South Carolina, ca. 1930.

The installation of Reverend D. Darrell Griffin *(kneeling),* pastor of the Antioch Baptist
Church, Brooklyn, New York, 1996.

Burial at Celestin family cemetery, Bobtown, Louisiana, 1982.

(Page 108)

At the Chicago Rail Station, Mamie Till Mobley sinks to her knees in prayer
at the arrival of the casket containing her murdered son, Emmett Louis Till, 1955.

(Page 111)

Getting the Spirit, Abyssinian Baptist Church, New York, New York, 1984.

(Page 113)

Nation of Islam, Los Angeles, California, 1990.

(Page 114)

The Church of God in Christ, Washington, D.C., 1942.

Gordon Parks, photographer, Library of Congress, Prints & Photographs Division,
reproduction number LC-USW3-010266-C

(Page 117)

From the photographer's Brooklyn Word Church series, Brooklyn, New York, 1988–89.

(Page 119)

Andrew Young leads prayer among Civil Rights marchers, Birmingham, Alabama, 1963.

(Page 121)

From the photographer's Brooklyn Word Church series, Brooklyn, New York, 1988–89.

(Page 122)

Young woman being converted at the Church of God in Christ, Washington, D.C., 1942.

Gordon Parks, photographer, Library of Congress, Prints & Photographs Division,
reproduction number LC-USW3-010261-C

(Page 125)

Holy Trinity Ethiopian Orthodox Tewahedo Church, Bronx, New York, 1990.

(Page 126)

A Muslim child raises his hands for prayers during the Eid Al-Fitr prayers
in Nairobi, Kenya, 2001, to mark the end of the holy month of Ramadan.

(Page 129)

Holy Trinity Ethiopian Orthodox Tewahedo Church, Bronx, New York, 1989.

(Page 130)

Former Washington, D.C., mayor Marion Barry is prayed over in a black church service
by church elders during his federal trial, Washington, D.C., 1993.

(Page 132)

Brother greeting brother, Spiritual Baptists in Barbados, 1988.

(Page 135)

A Buddhist prayer for peace, New York, New York, 2002.

(Page 137)

Rastafarian, Bull Bay, Jamaica, ca. 1990. The Rasta hand gesture is the reverential "Might of the Trinity"—a sign of the Father, Son, and Holy Ghost, as manifest to Rastafarians through the life of Emperor Haile Selassie of Ethiopia.

(Page 138)

From the photographer's Nation of Islam series, ca. 1963.

(Page 141)

Black Jewish Temple in Harlem, New York, New York, ca. 1940.

(Page 143)

A young soldier studies the Bible on the eve of the opening strike
of a raid on Manila Bay, January 9, 1945.

Courtesy National Archives, photo no. 80-G-30524

(Page 144)

From the photographer's storefront church series, ca. 1987.

(Page 147)

From the photographer's storefront church series, ca. 1987.

(Page 149)

Blowing the Shofar during the High Holy days at Commandment Keepers Synagogue, New York, New York, 1989. An ancient Hebrew instrument carved from a ram's horn, the Shofar was used to call assembly, signal sacrifice, or startle an enemy in battle. Today the Shofar is used at Rosh Hashanah (Jewish New Year) and Yom Kippur (the Day of Atonement).

In the invocation, HaShem means "the name" and is used to avoid saying Yahweh or Jehovah.

(Page 150)

From the photographer's Brooklyn Word Church series, Brooklyn, New York, 1988–89.

(Page 153)

The Reverend Dr. Martin Luther King, Jr., and his family pray before eating their Sunday dinner after church, Atlanta, Georgia, 1964.

(Page 154)

A man raises his hands in prayer during a song at a Promise Keepers rally in Veterans Stadium in Philadelphia, Pennsylvania, 1998.

(Page 157)

From the photographer's Nation of Islam series, ca. 1963.

(Page 158)

From the photographer's Remembrance and Ritual: A Tribute to the Ancestors of the Middle Passage series, entitled "Save a Space for Me . . . I'm On My Way," Brooklyn, New York, 1996.

(Page 160)

Church of God of Prophesy, the Bahamas, 1995.

(Page 163)

Southern University students pray for eighteen fellow students expelled for a lunch
counter sit-in, Louisiana, 1960. Hundreds attended the meeting,
which ended in mass prayer, and was held to give instructions for orderly mass
withdrawal from school in protest of expulsion of fellow students.

(Page 165)

From the photographer's Brooklyn Word Church series, Brooklyn, New York, 1988–89.

(Page 167)

Bishop Rebecca Belton of St. Ann's Assembly of Spiritualists in Harlem stands
before the altar of St. Anne, a Catholic saint considered to be the mother of Mary,
mother of Jesus, New York, New York, ca. 1950.

(Page 169)

Synagogue in Mount Vernon, New York, 1991.

(Page 170)

Reverend Jesse Jackson leads inmates in prayer during a visit to Cook County jail, Chicago, Illinois, 1997.

(Page 173)

From the photographer's Brooklyn Word Church series, Brooklyn, New York, 1988–89.

(Page 175)

From the photographer's Brooklyn Word Church series, Brooklyn, New York, 1988–89.

(Page 177)

Candomblé popcorn cleansing ritual for healing, a supplication to Omulu, the orixá or deity of contagious diseases, especially smallpox, Brazil, 1990.

Exu is the intermediary between humans and the supernatural orixás. Popcorn is part of the cleansing ritual to remove any negative energy in the invocation of the orixás and Exu, who is traditionally called upon first in Candomblé ceremonies. Considered a protector and guardian, Exu Tranca-Ruas means "Exu Who Locks Up the Streets."

(Page 179)

From the photographer's Brooklyn Word Church series, Brooklyn, New York, 1988–89.

(Page 181)

Saint Charles Borromeo Church in Harlem, New York, New York, ca. 1950.

(Page 182)

Evening prayers at a mosque in Brooklyn, New York, 1990.

(Page 185)

Sacred Heart Divine Temple, Brooklyn, New York, ca. 1985.

(Page 186)

From the photographer's Brooklyn Word Church series, Brooklyn, New York, 1988–89.

(Page 189)

From the photographer's storefront church series, ca. 1987.

(Page 190)

From the photographer's storefront church series, ca. 1987.

(Page 192)

Florence Griffith Joyner falls to her knees in a prayerful manner after taking the 200-meter Olympic final in world record time, Seoul, South Korea, 1988.

(Page 194)

Muslim World Day parade, New York, New York, 1999. The annual event draws Muslims from throughout the five boroughs.

(Page 197)

From the photographer's Brooklyn Word Church series, Brooklyn, New York, 1988–89.

(Page 198)

Two boys pray in front of the crypt of the Reverend Dr. Martin Luther King, Jr.,
during an interfaith prayer vigil for the World Trade Center at the King Center
in Atlanta, Georgia, 2001.

(Page 201)

Ordination of Archbishop Granville Williams, Spiritual Baptist in Barbados, 1987.

(Page 202)

Tent revival, St. Paul, Minnesota, 1984.

(Page 205)

A woman wearing a veil of mourning holds a card with the image of Amadou Diallo before the start of a prayer vigil outside the United Nations in New York, New York, 2000.

Diallo was shot forty-one times by New York City police officers in front of his home.

(Page 206)

A woman joins in song and prayer during a prayer rally at Mount Moriah Baptist Church, Los Angeles, California, September 11, 2001.

(Page 208)

Saint Martin's Spiritual Church, Washington, D.C., 1942.

Gordon Parks, photographer, Library of Congress, Prints & Photographs Division, reproduction number LC-USF34-013493-C

(Page 211)

From the photographer's Nation of Islam series, ca. 1963.

(Page 212)

A member of the Oblate Sisters of Providence in prayerful meditation, Catonsville, Maryland, ca. 1990. Founded in 1829 by Sister Mary Elisabeth Lange, a freed slave from the Dominican Republic, the order was the first to welcome women of color to the cloth.

(Page 215)

Worship service, South Carolina, ca. 1930.

(Page 216)

Performing the Kanaga Ceremony, a reenactment of the Dogon creation story,
Mali, 1993. In the cosmology of the Dogon people, the earth is female, and water is male.
The female or mother earth is the giver of life, love, sensuality, sustenance, and
prosperity. Similar beliefs are held in other African cultures, including the Akan.

(Page 219)

Pentecostal sunrise worship on the beach in Accra, Ghana, 1975.

P E R M I S S I O N S

Text on pages 8 and 91 reprinted from *Go Tell It on the Mountain* by James Baldwin. Copyright © 1981 by James Baldwin. Used by permission of Doubleday.

Text on pages 10 and 207 reprinted from *Poems of a Son, Prayers of a Father* by Matthew L. and William D. Watley, copyright © 1992 by Judson Press. Used by permission of Judson Press, 800-4-JUDSON, www.judsonpress.com.

Text on pages 13 and 20 reprinted from *Sister to Sister: Devotions for and from African American Women* by Suzan D. Johnson Cook, editor, copyright © 1995 by Judson Press. Used by permission of Judson Press, 800-4-JUDSON, www.judsonpress.com.

Text on page 16 reprinted from *When Roots Die: Endangered Traditions on the Sea Islands* by Patricia Jones-Jackson. Copyright © 1989 by The University of Georgia Press. Used by permission of The University of Georgia Press.

Text on pages 22, 124, and 218 from *The African Prayer Book*, selected and with introductions by Desmond Tutu, Doubleday, 1995. Used by permission of Doubleday.

"A Prayer for Healing the Body" by Reverend Lillie Kate Benitez on page 27, "In the Wake of Tragedy" by Chestina Mitchell Archibald on page 60, "My Prayer" by Mary McLeod Bethune on page 63, "Prayer of Healing" by Reverend Lillie Kate Benitez on page 115, and "A Prayer Against Injustice" by Dr. Mack King Carter on page 162, from *SAY AMEN!* by Chestina Mitchell Archibald, copyright © 1997 by The Philip Lief Group, Inc. Used by permission of Dutton, a division of Penguin Putnam Inc.

"A Prayer for Healing" by Richard Daniel Henton on page 28, from *Psalms in Black: A Study of Black Prayer in Three Diverse Contexts* by Frank B. Jones, thesis (Ph.D.), Indiana University, 1989.

I N D E X